PENGUIN BOOKS

REDISCOVERING JONAH

Timothy Keller was born and raised in Pennsylvania and educated at Bucknell University, Gordon-Conwell Theological Seminary, and Westminster Theological Seminary. He was first a pastor in Hopewell, Virginia. In 1989 he started Redeemer Presbyterian Church in New York City, with his wife, Kathy, and their three sons. Today, Redeemer has nearly six thousand regular Sunday attendees and has helped to start more than three hundred new churches around the world. In 2017 Keller moved from his role as senior minister at Redeemer to the staff of Redeemer City to City, an organization that helps national church leaders around the world reach and minister in global cities. He is the author of *God's Wisdom for Navigating Life*, *Hidden Christmas*, *Making Sense of God*, *The Meaning of Marriage*, *The Prodigal God*, and *The Reason for God*, as well as *On Birth*, *On Marriage*, and *On Death*, among others.

Praise for Timothy Keller and
Rediscovering Jonah

"Timothy Keller puts a contemporary spin on the familiar story of the prophet who disobeyed God and was swallowed by a whale."   —*Publishers Weekly*

"A Christian intellectual who takes on the likes of Nietzsche, Marx, and Freud."   —*The Wall Street Journal*

"Superb . . . We should be grateful to Keller for his wisdom, scholarship, and humility."
                                                        —The Gospel Coalition

"Tim Keller's ministry in New York City is leading a generation of seekers and skeptics toward belief in God. I thank God for him."   —Billy Graham

"Keller's work belongs on the bookshelf of every serious Bible student."   —Examiner.com

"Writing about philosophy and religion without jargon, condescension, or preaching, Keller produces an intelligent person's invitation to faith."   —*Booklist*

"Unlike most suburban megachurches, much of Redeemer is remarkably traditional. What is not traditional is Dr. Keller's skill in speaking the language of his urbane audience. . . . Observing Dr. Keller's professorial pose on stage, it is easy to understand his appeal." —*The New York Times*

"Fifty years from now, if evangelical Christians are widely known for their love of cities, their commitment to mercy and justice, and their love of their neighbors, Tim Keller will be remembered as a pioneer of the new urban Christians." —*Christianity Today*

"At Redeemer Presbyterian and in several books, Keller shaped a version of Evangelicalism that de-emphasizes politics and stresses care for the poor, personal sacrifice, and inclusiveness across ethnicity and class."
—*Fortune* (naming Timothy Keller one of the "World's 50 Greatest Leaders")

"In a flood of bestsellers by skeptics and atheists . . . Keller stands out as an effective counterpoint and a defender of the faith." —*The Washington Post*

"Keller provides a calm and measured invitation to examine convictions and assumptions in a way that both believers and skeptics could use as part of a reasoned dialogue." —*Library Journal*

REDISCOVERING JONAH

The Secret
of God's Mercy

TIMOTHY KELLER

Previously published as *The Prodigal Prophet*

PENGUIN BOOKS

PENGUIN BOOKS
An imprint of Penguin Random House LLC
penguinrandomhouse.com

First published in the United States of America as *The Prodigal Prophet* by Viking,
an imprint of Penguin Random House LLC, 2018
Published in Penguin Books 2020

ISBN 9780735222076 (paperback)

THE LIBRARY OF CONGRESS HAS CATALOGED THE
HARDCOVER EDITION AS FOLLOWS:
Names: Keller, Timothy, 1950– author.
Title: The prodigal prophet : Jonah and the mystery of God's mercy /
Timothy Keller.
Description: New York, New York : Viking, [2018] |
Includes bibliographical references.
Identifiers: LCCN 2018032868 | ISBN 9780735222069 (hardcover)
Subjects: LCSH: Bible. Jonah—Criticism, interpretation, etc. |
God (Christianity)—Mercy—Biblical teaching.
Classification: LCC BS1605.6.M436 K45 2018 | DDC 224/.9206—dc23
LC record available at https://lccn.loc.gov/2018032868

Printed in the United States of America
7   9   10   8   6

Designed by Gretchen Achilles

Passages from the book of Jonah were translated
by the author. All other Bible references are from the
New International Version (NIV), unless otherwise noted.

In gratitude to God for the life and ministry of

John Newton (1725–1807),

who also turned back to God during a storm,

and became a pastor who has taught us, and an untold

number of others,

the beauties of amazing grace

CONTENTS

❧

❧

PRODIGAL PROPHET

Like most people raised in a churchgoing home, I have been aware of the story of Jonah since childhood. As a minister who teaches the Bible, however, I have gone through several stages of puzzlement and wonder at this short book. The number of themes is a challenge for the interpreter. It seems to be about *so* many things.

Is it about race and nationalism, since Jonah seems to be more concerned over his nation's military security than over a city of spiritually lost people? Is it about God's call to mission, since Jonah at first flees from the call and later goes but regrets it? Is it about the struggles believers have to obey and trust in God? Yes to all those—and more. A mountain of scholarship exists about the book of Jonah that reveals the richness of the story, the many layers of meaning, and the varied applicability of it to so much of human life and thought.[1]

I discovered that "varied applicability" as I preached through the book of Jonah verse by verse three times in my ministry. The first time was at my first church in a small, blue-collar town in the South. Ten years later I preached through it to several hundred young, single professionals in Manhattan. Then, a decade after that, I preached through Jonah on the Sundays immediately after the 9/11 tragedy in New York City. In each case the audience's cultural location and personal needs were radically different, yet the text of Jonah was more than up to the task of powerfully addressing them. Many friends have told me over the years that the Jonah sermons they heard were life changing.

The narrative of Jonah seduces the reader into thinking of it as a simple fable, with the account of the great fish as the dramatic, if implausible, high point. Careful readers, however, find it to be an ingenious and artfully crafted work of literature. Its four chapters recount two incidents. In chapters 1 and 2 Jonah is given a command from God but fails to obey it; and in chapters 3 and 4 he is given the command again and this time carries it out. The two accounts are laid out in almost completely parallel patterns.

SCENE 1 *Jonah, the pagans, and the sea*	SCENE 2 *Jonah, the pagans, and the city*

JONAH AND GOD'S WORD

1:1 God's Word comes to Jonah	3:1 God's Word comes to Jonah
1:2 The message to be conveyed	3:2 The message to be conveyed
1:3 The response of Jonah	3:3 The response of Jonah

JONAH AND GOD'S WORLD

1:4 The word of warning	3:4 The word of warning
1:5 The response of the pagans	3:5 The response of the pagans
1:6 The response of the pagan leader	3:6 The response of the pagan leader
1:7ff How the pagans' response was ultimately better than Jonah's	3:7ff How the pagans' response was ultimately better than Jonah's

JONAH AND GOD'S GRACE

2:1–10 How God taught grace to Jonah through the fish	4:1–10 How God taught grace to Jonah through the plant

Despite the literary sophistication of the text, many modern readers still dismiss the work because the text tells us that Jonah was saved from the storm when swallowed by a "great fish" (Jonah 1:17). How you respond to this will depend on how you read the rest of the Bible. If you accept the existence of God and the resurrection of Christ (a far greater miracle), then there is nothing particularly difficult about reading Jonah literally. Certainly many people today believe all miracles are impossible, but that skepticism is just that—a belief that itself cannot be proven.[2] Not only that, but the text does not show evidence of the author having made up the miracle account. A fiction writer ordinarily adds supernatural elements in order to create excitement or spectacle and to capture reader attention, but this writer doesn't capitalize on the event at all in that way. The fish is mentioned only in two brief verses and there are no descriptive details. It is reported more as a simple fact of what happened.[3] So let's not get distracted by the fish.

The careful structure of the book reveals nuances of the author's message. Both episodes show how Jonah, a staunch religious believer, regards and relates to people who are racially and religiously different from him. The book of Jonah yields many insights about God's love for societies and people beyond the community of believers; about his opposition to toxic nationalism and disdain for other races; and about how to be "in mission" in the world despite the subtle and unavoidable power of idolatry in our own lives and hearts. Grasping these insights can make us bridge builders, peacemakers, and agents of reconciliation in the world. Such people are the need of the hour.

Yet to understand all of these lessons for our social relationships, we have to see that the book's main teaching is not sociological but theological. Jonah wants a God of his own making, a God who simply smites the bad people, for instance, the wicked Ninevites and blesses the good people, for instance, Jonah and his countrymen. When the real God—not Jonah's counterfeit—keeps showing up, Jonah is thrown into fury or despair. Jonah finds the real God to be an enigma because he cannot reconcile the mercy of God with his justice. How, Jonah asks, can God be merciful and forgiving to people who have done such violence and evil? How can God be *both* merciful and just?

That question is not answered in the book of Jonah. As part of the entire Bible, however, the book of Jonah is like a chapter that drives the Scripture's overall plotline forward. It teaches us to look ahead to how God saved the world through the one who called himself the ultimate Jonah (Matthew 12:41) so that he could be both just and the justifier of those who believe (Romans 3:26). Only when we readers fully grasp this gospel will we be neither cruel exploiters like the Ninevites nor Pharisaical believers like Jonah, but rather Spirit-changed, Christ-like women and men.

Many students of the book have noticed that in the first half Jonah plays the "prodigal son" of Jesus's famous parable (Luke 15:11–24), who ran from his father. In the second half of the book, however, Jonah is like the "older brother" (Luke 15:25–32), who obeys

his father but berates him for his graciousness to repentant sinners. The parable ends with a question
from the father to the Pharisaical son, just as the book
of Jonah ends with a question to the Pharisaical
prophet. There is a striking paralled between the two
stories, which Jesus himself may have had in mind.

༒

CHAPTER 1

RUNNING FROM GOD

[1] Now the Word of the LORD came to Jonah the son of Amittai, saying, [2] "Arise, go to Nineveh, that great city, and proclaim against her, for their evil has come up before my face." [3] But Jonah arose to flee to Tarshish from the face of the LORD.

—JONAH 1:1–3a[1]

The Unlikely Emissary

Our story begins when "the Word of the Lord came" to Jonah. This is the usual way to begin an account about one of the biblical prophets. God used them to convey his words and messages to Israel, especially in times of crisis. But already by verse 2 the original readers would have realized that this was a prophetic account unlike any that they had heard before. God called Jonah to go "to Nineveh, that great city, and proclaim . . ." This was stunning on several levels.

It was shocking first because it was a call for a Hebrew prophet to leave Israel and go out to a Gentile city. Up until then prophets had been sent only to God's people. While Jeremiah, Isaiah, and Amos all pronounced a few prophetic oracles addressed to pagan countries, they are brief, and none of those other men was actually sent out to the nations in order to preach. Jonah's mission was unprecedented.

It was even more shocking that the God of Israel would want to warn Nineveh, the capital of the Assyrian empire, of impending doom. Assyria was one of the cruelest and most violent empires of ancient times. Assyrian kings often recorded the results of their military victories, gloating of whole plains littered with corpses and of cities burned completely to the ground. The emperor Shalmaneser III is well known for depicting torture, dismembering, and decapitations of enemies in grisly detail on large stone relief panels. Assyrian history is "as gory and bloodcurdling a history as we know."[2] After capturing enemies, the Assyrians would typically cut off their legs and one arm, leaving the other arm and hand so they could shake the victim's hand in mockery as he was dying. They forced friends and family members to parade with the decapitated heads of their loved ones elevated on poles. They pulled out prisoners' tongues and stretched their bodies with ropes so they could be flayed alive and their skins displayed on city walls. They burned adolescents alive.[3] Those who survived the destruction of their cities were fated to endure cruel and violent forms of slavery. The Assyrians have been called a "terrorist state."[4]

The empire had begun exacting heavy tribute from Israel during the reign of King Jehu (842–815 BC) and continued to threaten the Jewish northern kingdom throughout the lifetime of Jonah. In 722 BC it finally invaded and destroyed the northern kingdom of Israel and its capital, Samaria.

Yet it was this nation that was the object of God's missionary outreach. Though God told Jonah to "proclaim against" the city for its wickedness, there would have been no reason to send a warning unless there was a chance of judgment being averted, as Jonah knew very well (4:1–2). But how could a good God give a nation like that even the merest chance to experience his mercy? Why on earth would God be helping the enemies of his people?

Perhaps the most surprising element of this narrative was who it was that God chose to send. It was "Jonah the son of Amittai." No background information is given, meaning he needed no introduction. 2 Kings 14:25 tells us Jonah ministered during the reign of Israel's King Jeroboam II (786–746 BC). In that text we learn that, unlike the prophets Amos and Hosea, who criticized the royal administration for its injustice and unfaithfulness, Jonah had supported Jeroboam's aggressive military policy to extend the nation's power and influence. The original readers of the book of Jonah would have remembered him as intensely patriotic, a highly partisan nationalist.[5] And they would have been amazed that God would send a man like that to preach to the very people he most feared and hated.

Nothing about this mission made any sense. Indeed,

it seemed almost to be an evil plot. If any Israelite had come up with this idea, he would have been at least shunned and at worst executed. How could God have asked anyone to betray his country's interests like this?

Refusing God

In a deliberate parody of God's call to "arise, go to Nineveh," Jonah "arose" to go in the opposite direction (verse 3). Tarshish, it is believed, lay on the outermost western rim of the world known to Israelites of the time.[6] In short, Jonah did the exact opposite of what God told him to do. Called to go east, he went west. Directed to travel overland, he went to sea. Sent to the big city, he bought a one-way ticket to the end of the world.

Why did he refuse? A full accounting of Jonah's reasoning and motives must wait for Jonah's own words later in the book. But at this point, the text invites us to make some guesses. We can certainly imagine that Jonah thought the mission made neither practical nor theological sense.

God describes Nineveh both here and later as that "great" city, and indeed it was. It was both a military and a cultural powerhouse. Why would the populace listen to someone like Jonah? How long, for example, would a Jewish rabbi have lasted in 1941 if he had stood on the streets of Berlin and called on Nazi Germany to repent? At the most practical level, the prospects of success were none, and the chances of death were high.

Jonah would not have been able to see any theological justification for this mission either. The prophet Nahum had some years before prophesied that God would destroy Nineveh for its evil.[7] Jonah and Israel would have accepted Nahum's prediction as making perfect sense. Wasn't Israel God's chosen, loved people through whom he was fulfilling his purposes in the world? Wasn't Nineveh an evil society on a collision course with the Lord? Wasn't Assyria unusually violent and oppressive, even for its time? Of course God would destroy it—that was obvious and (Jonah would have thought) settled. Why, then, this call to Jonah? Wouldn't a successful mission to Nineveh only destroy God's own promises to Israel and prove Nahum a false prophet? What possible justification, then, could there be for this assignment?

Mistrusting God

So Jonah had a problem with the job he was given. But he had a bigger problem with the One who gave it to him.[8] Jonah concluded that because he could not see any good reasons for God's command, there couldn't be any. Jonah doubted the goodness, wisdom, and justice of God.

We have all had that experience. We sit in the doctor's office stunned by the biopsy report. We despair of ever finding decent employment after the last lead has dried up. We wonder why the seemingly perfect romantic relationship—the one we always wanted and never thought was possible—has crashed and burned. If there is a God, we think, he doesn't know what he is doing! Even when we turn from the circumstances of our lives to the teaching of the Bible itself, it seems, to modern people especially, to be filled with claims that don't make much sense.

When this happens we have to decide—does God know what's best, or do we? And the default mode of the unaided human heart is to always decide that *we* do. We doubt that God is good, or that he is committed to our happiness, and therefore if we can't see any good reasons for something God says or does, we assume that there aren't any.

That's what Adam and Eve did in the Garden. The first divine command was: "And the LORD God commanded the man, 'You are free to eat from any tree in the garden, but you must not eat from the tree of the knowledge of good and evil, for when you eat from it you will certainly die'" (Genesis 2:16–17). There was the fruit, and it looked very "good . . . pleasing . . . and desirable" (Genesis 3:6), yet God had given no *reason* as to why it would be wrong to eat. Adam and Eve, like Jonah many years later, decided that if they couldn't think of a good reason for a command of God, there couldn't be one. God could not be trusted to have their best interests in mind. And so they ate.

Two Ways of Running from God

Jonah runs away from God. But if we for a moment stand back and look at the entirety of the book, Jonah will teach us that there are two different strategies for escaping from God. Paul outlines these in Romans 1–3.

First Paul speaks of those who simply reject God overtly and "have become filled with every kind of wickedness, evil, greed and depravity" (Romans 1:29). In chapter 2, however, he talks of those who seek to follow the Bible. "You rely on the law and boast . . . in God. . . . You know his will and approve of what is superior because you are instructed by the law" (Romans 2:17–18). Then, after looking at both pagan, immoral Gentiles and Bible-believing, moral Jews, he concludes in a remarkable summation "that there is no one righteous, not even one. . . . All have turned away" (Romans 3:10–12). One group is trying diligently to follow God's law and the other ignores it, and yet Paul says *both* have "turned away." They are both, in different ways, running from God. We all know that we can run from God by becoming immoral and irreligious. But Paul is saying it is also possible to avoid God by becoming *very* religious and moral.

The classic example in the gospels of these two ways to run from God is in Luke 15, the parable of the two sons.[9] The younger brother tried to escape his father's control by taking his inheritance, leaving home, rejecting all his father's moral values, and living as he wished. The older brother stayed home and obeyed the father completely, but when his father did something with the remaining wealth that the older son disliked, he exploded in anger at his father. At that point it became obvious that he, also, did not love his father.

The elder brother was not obeying out of love but only as a way, he thought, of putting his father in his debt, getting control over him so he had to do as his older son asked. Neither son trusted his father's love. Both were trying to find ways of escaping his control. One did it by obeying all the father's rules, the other by disobeying them all.

Flannery O'Connor describes one of her fictional characters, Hazel Motes, as knowing that "the way to avoid Jesus was to avoid sin."[10] We think that if we are religiously observant, virtuous, and good, then we've paid our dues, as it were. Now God can't just ask anything of us—he owes us. He is obligated to answer our prayers and bless us. This is not moving toward him in grateful joy, glad surrender, and love, but is instead a way of controlling God and, as a result, keeping him at arm's length.

Both of these two ways of escaping God assume the lie that we cannot trust God's commitment to our good. We think we have to force God to give us what we need. Even if we are outwardly obeying God, we are doing it not for his sake but for ours. If, as we seek to comply with his rules, God does not appear to be treating us as we feel we deserve, then the veneer of morality and righteousness can collapse overnight.

The inward distancing from God that had been going on for a long time becomes an outward, obvious rejection. We become furious with God and just walk away.

The classic Old Testament example of these two ways to run from God is right here in the book of Jonah. Jonah takes turns acting as both the "younger brother" and the "older brother." In the first two chapters of the book, Jonah disobeys and runs away from the Lord and yet ultimately repents and asks for God's grace, just as the younger brother leaves home but returns repentant.

In the last two chapters, however, Jonah obeys God's command to go and preach to Nineveh. In both cases, however, he's trying to get control of the agenda.[11] When God accepts the repentance of the Ninevites, just like the older brother in Luke 15, Jonah bristles with self-righteous anger at God's graciousness and mercy to sinners.[12]

And that is the problem facing Jonah, namely, the mystery of God's mercy. It is a theological problem, but it is at the same time a heart problem. Unless

Jonah can see his own sin, and see himself as living wholly by the mercy of God, he will never understand how God can be merciful to evil people and still be just and faithful. The story of Jonah, with all its twists and turns, is about how God takes Jonah, sometimes by the hand, other times by the scruff of the neck, to show him these things.

Jonah runs and runs. But even though he uses multiple strategies, the Lord is always a step ahead. God varies his strategies too, and continually extends mercy to us in new ways, even though we neither understand nor deserve it.

❦

CHAPTER 2

THE WORLD'S STORMS

³ He went down to Joppa and, finding a ship bound for Tarshish, he paid the fare and went down into it, to go with them to Tarshish, away from the face of the LORD. ⁴ But the LORD hurled a great wind upon the sea, and there was such a mighty tempest that the ship expected to break up.

—JONAH 1:3b–4

Jonah runs but God won't let him go. The Lord "hurled a great wind upon the sea" (verse 4). The word "hurled" is often used for throwing a weapon such as a spear (1 Samuel 18:11). It is a vivid picture of God launching a mighty tempest onto the sea around Jonah's boat. It was a "great" (*gedola*) wind—the same word used to describe Nineveh. If Jonah refuses to go into a great city, he will go into a great storm. From this we learn both dismaying and comforting news.

Storms Attached to Sin

The dismaying news is that every act of disobedience to God has a storm attached to it. This is one of the great themes of the Old Testament wisdom literature, especially the book of Proverbs. We must be careful here. This is not to say that every difficult thing that comes into our lives is the punishment for some particular sin. The entire book of Job contradicts the common belief that good people will have lives that go well, and that if your life is going badly, it must be your fault. The Bible does not say that every difficulty is the result of sin—but it does teach that every sin will bring you into difficulty.

We cannot treat our bodies indifferently and still expect to have good health. We cannot treat people indifferently and expect to maintain their friendship.

We cannot all put our own selfish interests ahead of the common good and still have a functioning society. If we violate the design and purpose of things—if we sin against our bodies, our relationships, or society— they strike back. There are consequences. If we violate the laws of God, we are violating our own design, since God built us to know, serve, and love him. The Bible speaks sometimes about God punishing sin ("The Lord detests all the proud of heart. . . . They will not go unpunished," Proverbs 16:5) but some other times of the sin itself punishing us ("The violence of the wicked will drag them away, for they refuse to do what is right," Proverbs 21:7). Both are true at once. All sin has a storm attached to it.

Old Testament scholar Derek Kidner writes: "Sin . . . sets up strains in the structure of life which can only end in breakdown."[1] Generally speaking, liars are lied to, attackers are attacked, and he who lives by the sword dies by the sword. God created us to live for him more than for anything else, so there is a spiritual "givenness" to our lives. If we build our lives and meaning on anything more than God, we are acting against the grain of the universe and of our own design and therefore of our own being.

Here the results of Jonah's disobedience are immediate and dramatic. There is a mighty storm directed right at Jonah. Its suddenness and fury are something even the pagan sailors can discern as being of supernatural origin. That is not the norm, however. The results of sin are often more like the physical response you have to a debilitating dose of radiation. You don't suddenly feel pain the moment you are exposed. It isn't like a bullet or sword tearing into you. You feel quite normal. Only later do you experience symptoms, but by then it is too late.

Sin is a suicidal action of the will upon itself. It is like taking an addicting drug. At first it may feel wonderful, but every time it gets harder to not do it again. Here's just one example. When you indulge yourself in bitter thoughts, it feels so satisfying to fantasize about payback. But slowly and surely it will enlarge your capacity for self-pity, erode your ability to trust and enjoy relationships, and generally drain the happiness out of your daily life. Sin always hardens the conscience, locks you in the prison of your own defensiveness and rationalizations, and eats you up slowly from the inside.

All sin has a mighty storm attached to it. The image is powerful because even in our technologically advanced society, we cannot control the weather. You cannot bribe a storm or baffle it with logic and rhetoric. "You will be sinning against the Lord, and you may be sure that your sin will find you out" (Numbers 32:23).

Storms Attached to Sinners

The dismaying news is that sin always has a storm attached to it, but there is comforting news too. For Jonah the storm was the consequence of his sin, yet the sailors were caught in it too. Most often the storms of life come upon us not as the consequence of a particular sin but as the unavoidable consequence of living in a fallen, troubled world. It has been said that "man is born to trouble as surely as sparks fly upward" (Job 5:7), and therefore the world is filled with destructive storms. Yet as we will see, this storm leads the sailors to genuine faith in the true God even though it was not their fault. Jonah himself begins his journey to understand the grace of God in a new way. When storms come into our lives, whether as a consequence of our wrongdoing or not, Christians have the promise that God will use them for their good (Romans 8:28).

When God wanted to make Abraham into a man of faith who could be the father of all the faithful on earth, he put him through years of wandering with apparently unfulfilled promises. When God wanted to turn Joseph from an arrogant, deeply spoiled teenager into a man of character, he put him through years of rough handling. He had to experience slavery and imprisonment before he could save his people. Moses had to become a fugitive and spend forty years in the lonely wilderness before he could lead.

The Bible does not say that every difficulty is the result of our sin—but it does teach that, for Christians, every difficulty can help reduce the power of sin over our hearts. Storms can wake us up to truths we would otherwise never see. Storms can develop faith, hope, love, patience, humility, and self-control in us that nothing else can. And innumerable people have testified that they found faith in Christ and eternal life only because some great storm drove them toward God.

Again, we must tread carefully. The first chapters of Genesis teach that God did not create the world and the human race for suffering, disease, natural disasters, aging, and death. Evil entered the world when we turned away from him. God has tied his heart to us such that when he sees the sin and suffering in the world his heart is filled with pain (Genesis 6:6) and "in all [our] affliction he too [is] afflicted" (Isaiah 63:9).[2] God is not like a chess player casually moving us pawns around on a board. Nor is it usually clear until years later, if ever in this life, what good God was accomplishing in the difficulties we suffered.

How God Works Through Storms

Nevertheless, as hard as it is to discern God's loving and wise purposes behind many of our trials and difficulties, it would be even more hopeless to imagine that he has no control over them or that our sufferings are random and meaningless.

Jonah could not see that deep within the terror of the storm God's mercy was at work, drawing him back to change his heart. It's not surprising that Jonah missed this initially. He did not know how God would come into the world to save us. We, however, living on this side of the cross, know that God can save through weakness, suffering, and apparent defeat. Those who watched Jesus dying saw nothing but loss and tragedy. Yet at the heart of that darkness the divine mercy was powerfully at work, bringing about pardon and forgiveness for us. God's salvation came into the world through suffering, so his saving grace and power can work in our lives more and more as we go through difficulty and sorrow. There's mercy deep inside our storms.

CHAPTER 3

୧୨୬

WHO IS MY NEIGHBOR?

⁵ Then the mariners were terrified, and each cried out to his gods. Then they hurled the equipment in the ship into the sea to lighten it. But Jonah went down into the hold of the ship, lay down, and fell into a deep sleep. ⁶ Then the captain of the mariners came to him and said, "How can you be sleeping? Arise, call out to your god! Perhaps the god will favor us, that we may not perish."

—JONAH 1:5–6

The book of Jonah is divided into two symmetrical halves—the records of Jonah's flight from God and then of his mission to Nineveh. Each part has three sections—God's word to Jonah, then his encounter with the Gentile pagans, and finally Jonah talking to God. Twice, then, Jonah finds himself in a close encounter with people who are racially and religiously different. In both cases his behavior is dismissive and unhelpful, while the pagans uniformly act more admirably than he does. This is one of the main messages of the book, namely, that God cares how we believers relate to and treat people who are deeply different from us.

Preachers and teachers of the book usually overlook these sections, except perhaps to observe that we should be willing to take the gospel to foreign lands. That is certainly true, but it misses the fuller meaning of Jonah's interactions with the pagans. God wants us to treat people of different races and faiths in a way that is respectful, loving, generous, and just.

Jonah and the Sailors

Jonah had rejected God's call to preach to Nineveh. He did not want to talk to pagans about God or to lead them toward faith. So he fled—only to find himself talking about God to the exact sort of people he was fleeing!

When the fierce storm began, "the mariners were terrified" (verse 5). These were experienced sailors who took bad weather in stride, so this must have been a uniquely terrifying tempest. Yet Jonah is deep in the hold of the ship, sleeping soundly. The nineteenth-century Scottish minister Hugh Martin says Jonah was sleeping "the sleep of sorrow." Many of us know exactly what that is—the desire to escape reality through sleep, even for a little while.[1] He was profoundly spent and exhausted, drained by powerful emotions of anger, guilt, anxiety, and grief.

This is one of several carefully laid out contrasts between the despised pagan sailors and the morally respectable prophet of Israel. While Jonah is out of touch with his peril, the sailors are extremely alert. While Jonah is thoroughly absorbed by his own problems, they are seeking the common good of everyone in the boat. They pray each to their own god, but Jonah does not pray to his. They are also spiritually aware enough to sense that this is not just a random storm but of peculiar intensity. Perhaps it appeared with suddenness not attributable to natural forces. They are astute enough to conclude that the tempest is of divine origin, possibly a response to someone's grave sin.[2] Finally, they are not narrow and bigoted. They are open to calling on Jonah's God. In fact, they are more ready to do this than he is.

When the captain finds the sleeping prophet he says, "Arise, call . . . !" (Hebrew *qum lek*, verse 6), the same words God used when calling Jonah to arise, go, and call Nineveh to repentance.[3] But as Jonah rubs his eyes there is a Gentile mariner with God's very words in *his* mouth. What is this? God sent his prophet to point the pagans toward himself. Yet now it is the pagans pointing the prophet toward God.

The sailors continue to act in commendable ways. Discerning that there is human sin and a divine hand behind the storm, they cast lots. Casting lots in order to discern the divine will was quite common in ancient times. It is possible that each man's name was put on a stick, and the one that was chosen was Jonah's.[4] God uses the lot casting, in this case, to point the finger at Jonah. Yet even now, when they seem to have divine guidance, the sailors do not panic and immediately lay angry hands on him. They don't assume that they now have a mandate to kill him. Instead they carefully take his evidence and testimony in order to make the right decision. They show him and his God the greatest of respect. Even when Jonah proposes that they throw him overboard, they do everything possible to avoid doing it. At every point they outshine Jonah.

There is much here in this part of the story that its author wants us to see. What should Jonah have been learning—and what should we?

Seeking the Common Good

First, we learn that people outside the community of faith have a right to evaluate the church on its commitment to the good of all.

The sailors are in peril. They have used what technology and religious resources they have, but these are not enough. They sense that they cannot be saved without help from Jonah, but he is doing nothing to help. And so we have this memorable picture of the heathen captain reprimanding God's holy prophet. Hugh Martin preached a sermon on this text entitled "The World Rebuking the Church"[5] and concluded that Jonah deserved it and, to a great extent, the church today deserves it too.

What is the captain rebuking Jonah for? It is because he has no interest in their common good. The captain is saying: "Can't you see we're about to die? How can you be so oblivious to our need? I understand you are a man of faith. Why aren't you using your faith for the public good?" Jacques Ellul writes:

> These Joppa sailors . . . are pagans, or, in modern terms, non-Christians. But . . . the lot of non-Christians and Christians is . . . linked; they are in the same boat. The safety of all depends on what each does. . . . They are in the same storm, subject to the same peril, and they want the same outcome . . . and this ship typifies our situation.[6]

We are all—believers and nonbelievers—"in the same boat." (Never was that old saying truer than it was for Jonah!) If crime plagues a community, or poor health, or a water shortage, or the loss of jobs, if an economy and social order is broken, we are all in the same boat. For a moment, Jonah lives in the same "neighborhood" with these sailors, and the storm that threatens one person threatens the entire community. Jonah fled because he did *not* want to work for the good of the pagans—he wanted to serve exclusively the interests of believers. But God shows him here that he is the God of all people and Jonah needs to see himself as being part of the whole human community, not only a member of a faith community.

This is not a merely pragmatic argument: "Believers had better help nonbelievers or things will not go well with them." The Bible tells us we are co-humans with all people—made in God's image and therefore infinitely precious to him (Genesis 9:6; James 3:9).

The captain urges Jonah to do what he can for them all. Of course, the captain has no accurate ideas about Jonah's God. He is probably hoping only for a prayer to some powerful supernatural being. Yet, as Hugh Martin argues, the criticism is still true. Jonah is not bringing the resources of his faith to bear on the suffering of his fellow citizens. He is not telling them how to get a relationship with the God of the universe. Nor is he, relying on his own spiritual resources in God, simply loving and serving the practical needs of his neighbors. God commands all believers to do both things, but he is doing neither. His private faith is of no public good.

Someone might object that the world has no right to rebuke the church, but there is biblical warrant for doing exactly that. In Jesus's Sermon on the Mount he said that the world would see the good deeds of believers and glorify God (Matthew 5:16). The world will not see who our Lord is if we do not live as we ought. In the words of one book we are "The Church Before the Watching World."[7] We deserve the critique of the world if the church does not exhibit visible love in practical deeds. The captain had every right to rebuke a believer who was oblivious to the problems of the people around him and doing nothing for them.

Recognizing Common Grace

We also learn that believers are to respect and learn from the wisdom God gives to those who don't believe. The pagan sailors provide a graphic portrayal of what theologians have called "common grace."

> In [this] episode, hope, justice, and integrity reside not with Jonah . . . but with the captain and the sailors. . . . Though blameless victims, the sailors never cry injustice. Finding themselves in a dangerous situation not of their making, they seek to solve it for the good of all. Never do they wallow in self-pity, berate an angry god . . . condemn an arbitrary world, target the culprit Jonah for vengeance, or promote violence as an answer.[8]

The doctrine of common grace is the teaching that God bestows gifts of wisdom, moral insight, goodness, and beauty across humanity, regardless of race or religious belief. James 1:17 says, "Every good and perfect gift is from above, coming down from the Father of the heavenly lights." That is, God is ultimately enabling every act of goodness, wisdom, justice, and beauty—no matter who does it. Isaiah 45:1 speaks of Cyrus, a pagan king, whom God anoints and uses for world leadership. Isaiah 28:23–29 tells us that when a farmer is fruitful, it is God who has been teaching him to be so.

That means that all good and great artistic expressions, skillful farming, effective governments, and scientific advances are God's gifts to the human race. They are undeserved, gifts of God's mercy and grace. They are also "common." That is, they are distributed to any and all. There is no indication that the monarch or the farmer mentioned in Isaiah embraced God by faith. Common grace does not regenerate the heart, save the soul, or create a personal, covenant relationship with God. Yet without it the world would be an intolerable place to live. It is wonderful expression of God's love to all people (Psalm 145:14–16).

Certainly common grace was staring Jonah right in the face. Jonah himself was a recipient of what has been called "special grace." He had received the Word of God, a revelation of his will not available to human reason or wisdom, however great. Jonah was a follower of the Lord, the true God. So how was it possible that the pagans were outshining Jonah? Common grace means that nonbelievers often act more righteously than believers despite their lack of faith; whereas believers, filled with remaining sin, often act far worse than their right belief in God would lead us to expect. All this means Christians should be humble and respectful toward those who do not share their faith. They should be appreciative of the work of all people, knowing that nonbelievers have many things to teach them. Jonah is learning this the hard way.

Who Is My Neighbor?

Both of these insights about the importance of common grace and the common good are taught in Jesus's famous parable of the Good Samaritan (Luke 10:25–37). Jesus takes the seemingly pedestrian exhortation "love thy neighbor" and gives it the most radical possible definition. He tells us that all in need, including those of other races and beliefs, are our neighbors. We are also shown that the way to "love" neighbors is not merely through sentiment but through costly, sacrificial, practical action to meet material and economic needs.

The text indicates that Jonah resisted doing anything or even talking to the pagan sailors. The bad prophet, Jonah, is the very opposite of the Good Samaritan. He has no concern for the "common good," no respect for the nonbelievers around him. In the New Testament book of James, the author argues that if you say you have a relationship with God based on his grace, and you see someone "without clothes and daily food" (James 2:15) and do nothing about it, you only prove that your faith is "dead"—unreal (verse 17).[9] That is why James can say, "Judgment without mercy will be shown to anyone who has not been merciful" (verse 13). The lack of mercy in Jonah's attitude and actions toward others reveals that he was a stranger in his heart to the saving mercy and grace of God.

CHAPTER 4

ᘓᕈᖆᕬ

EMBRACING THE OTHER

[7] *And they said to one another, "Come, let us cast lots, that we may know who is responsible for this calamity that has come upon us." So they cast lots, and the lot fell on Jonah.* [8] *Then they said to him, "Speak to us, you who are responsible for this evil which is come upon us. What is your mission and from where do you come? What is your country and of which people do you belong?"* [9] *And he said to them, "I am a Hebrew, and the LORD, the God of heaven, who made the sea and the dry land—he is the one I fear."* [10] *Then the men were seized by a great fear and—after he admitted that he was fleeing from the face of the Lord—they said to him: "How could you have done this!"*

—JONAH 1:7–10

Who Are You?

The sailors conclude that the storm was a punishment for sin, and they cast lots to discover whose wrongdoing it might be. When the lots indicate Jonah, they begin to pepper him with questions. Essentially they were asking three things—his purpose (*what is your mission?*), his place (*from where do you come? what is your country?*), and his race (*who are your people?*).[1]

These are identity questions. Every person's identity has multiple aspects. "Who are your people?" probes the social aspect. We define ourselves not only as individuals but also by the community (family, racial group, political party) with which we identify most closely. "Where do you come from?" points to the physical place and space in which we are most at home, where we feel we belong. "What is your mission?" gets at our meaning in life. All people do many things—work, rest, marry, travel, create—but what are we doing it all *for*? All of these provide an identity, a sense of significance and security.

A few years ago I met Mike. When I asked him who he was, he told me he was an Irishman who had lived in the U.S. for twenty years, having moved here to get a good job. He worked in construction and so was able to provide for and raise his family, which was the "main thing I am about," Mike said. However, he hoped to return to Ireland eventually because that was where he felt most at home. I also met his son, Robert, a newly minted lawyer who worked for a nonprofit that represented people who lived in low-income housing.

Using questions about mission, place, and people, it was possible to see how there had been an identity shift between the generations. Everyone's identity consists of layers. Robert's job was the most foundational layer of his identity. Being a trained professional and doing justice for the poor was the real meaning of his life. When I spoke to him at the time, he had little interest in marriage or family, being so absorbed in his work. Mike's job, on the other hand, was not his most foundational layer. It was merely a source of money for his main mission in life, namely, being a good provider and raising his family. While Robert valued his Irish roots, he had no intention of moving to Ireland. The U.S. was his place. This father and son both had identities consisting of mission, place, and race, but they ordered them differently.

These questions of the sailors show a good understanding of how we constitute our identity. To ask about purpose, place, and people is an insightful way of asking, "Who are you?"

Whose Are You?

The sailors, however, are not asking these questions simply to let Jonah express himself, as we do in modern Western culture. Their urgent goal is to understand the God who has been angered so they can determine what they should do. In ancient times, every racial group, every place, and even every profession had its own god or gods. To find out which deity Jonah had offended, they did not need to ask, "What is your god's name?" All they had to ask was who he was. In their minds, human identity factors were inextricably linked to what you worshipped. Who you were and what you worshipped were just two sides of the same coin. It was the most foundational layer of your identity.

Today we may be tempted to say something like "People no longer believe in the gods and often don't believe in any god at all. So this superstitious view— that your identity is rooted in what you worship—is irrelevant today." To say this is to commit a fundamental error.

Certainly Christians would agree that there are not multiple, personal, conscious, supernatural beings attached to every profession, place, and race. There is no actual Roman god named Mercury, the god of commerce, to whom we should burn animal sacrifices. Yet no one doubts that financial profit can become a god, an unquestioned ultimate goal for either an individual life or a whole society, to which persons and moral standards and relationships and communities are sacrificed. And while there is no Venus, goddess of beauty, nevertheless untold numbers of men and women are obsessed with body image or enslaved to an unrealizable idea of sexual fulfillment.

Therefore, the sailors are not wrong in their analysis. Everyone gets an identity from something. Everyone must say to himself or herself, "I'm significant because of *This*" and "I'm acceptable because I'm welcomed by *Them*." But then whatever *This is* and whoever *They are*, these things become virtual gods to us, and the deepest truths about who we are. They become things we *must* have under any circumstances. I recently spoke to a man who had been in meetings in which a financial institution decided to invest in a new technology. Privately, the individuals in the room admitted to him that they had real reservations about the effect of the technology on society. They thought it would eliminate many jobs for every one new job it produced, and that it might be bad for the youth who would primarily use it. But to walk away from the deal would have meant leaving billions of dollars on the table. And no one could imagine doing that. When financial success commands allegiance that is unconditional and that cannot be questioned, it functions as a religious object, a god, even a "salvation."[2]

The Bible explains why this is the case. We were made in "the image of God" (Genesis 1:26–27). There can be no image without an original of which the image is a reflection. "To be in the image" means that human beings were not created to stand alone. We must get our significance and security from something of ultimate value outside us. To be created in God's image means we must live for the true God or we will have to make something else God and orbit our lives around that.[3]

The sailors knew that identity is always rooted in the things we look toward to save us, the things to which we give ultimate allegiance. To ask, "Who are you?" is to ask, "Whose are you?" To know who you are is to know what you have given yourself to, what controls you, what you most fundamentally trust.

Spiritually Shallow Identity

Jonah finally begins to speak. In the boat he has stayed as withdrawn from the unclean pagans as he could. When the captain urges him to pray to his God,

Jonah responds with silence. Only when the lot is cast and the entire ship confronts Jonah do we finally get a response from the reluctant prophet.

Though the question about race comes last in the list, Jonah answers it first. "I am a Hebrew," he says before anything else. In a text so sparing with words, it is significant that he reverses the order and puts his race out front as the most significant part of his identity. As we have seen, an identity has several aspects or layers, some of which are more fundamental to the person than others. As one scholar put it, "Since Jonah identifies himself first ethnically, then religiously, we may infer that his ethnicity is foremost in his self-identity."[4]

While Jonah had faith in God, it appears not to have been as deep and fundamental to his identity as his race and nationality. Many people in the world tack on their religion, as it were, to their ethnic identity, which is more foundational for them. Someone might say, for example, "Why, of course I'm Lutheran—I'm Norwegian!" even though she never attends church at all.

If his race was more foundational to his self-image

than his faith, it begins to explain why Jonah was so opposed to calling Nineveh to repentance. The prospect of calling people of other nations to faith in God would not be appealing under any circumstances to someone with this spiritually shallow identity. Jonah's relationship with God was not as basic to his significance as his race. That is why, when loyalty to his people and loyalty to the Word of God seemed to be in conflict, he chose to support his nation over taking God's love and message to a new society.

Unfortunately, many Christians today exhibit the same attitudes. This is not merely the result of poor education or cultural narrowness. Rather, their relationship with God through Christ has not gone deep enough into their heart. Just as in Jonah's life, God and his love is not their identity's most fundamental layer. Of course, race is not the only thing that can block the development of a Christian self-understanding. For example, you may sincerely believe that Jesus died for your sins, and yet your significance and security can be far more grounded in your career and financial worth than in the love of God through Christ.

Shallow Christian identities explain why professing Christians can be racists and greedy materialists, addicted to beauty and pleasure, or filled with anxiety and prone to overwork. All this comes because it is not Christ's love but the world's power, approval, comfort, and control that are the real roots of our self-identity.

A Self-Blinding Identity

A shallow identity is also one that prevents us from truly seeing ourselves. Here is Jonah, a prophet of God with a privileged position in the covenant community, who is at every turn obtuse, self-absorbed, bigoted, and foolish. Yet he doesn't seem aware of it at all. Indeed, he seems more blind to his flaws than anyone around him. How can this be?

Jonah reminds us of another biblical figure—Peter. He also had a position of privilege in the faith community. He was one of the intimate friends of Jesus himself, and he was quite proud of the fact. Before Jesus's arrest, Peter swore that, if persecution came, though the other disciples might abandon Jesus, he would not do so (John 13:37; Matthew 26:35). He said, in effect, "My love and devotion for you is stronger than any of the other disciples'. I'll be braver than everyone else, no matter what happens." But he turned out to be a greater coward than the rest, denying Jesus publicly three times. How could Peter have been so blind to who he was?

The answer is that Peter's most fundamental identity was not rooted as much in Jesus's gracious love for him as it was in *his* commitment and love to Jesus. His self-regard was rooted in the level of commitment to Christ that he thought he had achieved. He was confident before God and humanity because, he thought, he was a fully devoted follower of Christ. There are two results of such an identity.

The first is blindness to one's real self. If you get your sense of worth from how courageous you are, it will be traumatic to admit to any cowardice at all.

If your very self is based on your valor, any failure of nerve would mean there would be no "you" left. You would feel you had no worth at all. Indeed, if you base your identity on any kind of achievement, goodness, or virtue, you will have to live in denial of the depth of your faults and shortcomings. You won't have an identity secure enough to admit your sins, weaknesses, and flaws.

The second result is hostility, rather than respect, for people who are different. When they came to arrest Jesus, even though Jesus had told them numerous times that this had to happen, Peter pulled out a sword and cut off the ear of one of the soldiers. Any identity based on your own achievement and performance is an insecure one. You are never sure you have done enough. That means, on the one hand, that you cannot be honest with yourself about your own flaws. But it also means that you always need to reinforce it by contrasting yourself with—and being hostile to—those who are different.

Peter and Jonah were proud of their religious devotion

and based their self-image on their spiritual achievements. As a result they were both blind to their flaws and sins and hostile to those who were different. Jonah shows no concern for the spiritual plight of the Ninevites, nor any interest in working together with the pagan sailors for the good of all. He treats the pagans not just as different but as "other"—and he is engaging in several kinds of exclusion.

An Excluding Identity

What Jonah is doing is what some have called *othering*. To categorize people as *the Other* is to focus on the ways they are different from oneself, to focus on their strangeness and to reduce them to these characteristics until they are dehumanized. We then can say, "You know how *they* are," so we don't need to engage with them. This makes it possible to exclude them in various ways—by simply ignoring them, or by forcing them to conform to our beliefs and practices, or by requiring them to live in certain poor neighborhoods, or by just driving them out.[5]

We readers are by now beginning to see that Jonah is in desperate need of the very mercy of God that he finds so troubling. Under the power of God's grace his identity will have to change, as will ours.

❧

CHAPTER 5

THE PATTERN OF LOVE

[11] *Then they said to him, "What must we do to you, that the sea may become quiet for us, for the sea is more and more tempestuous?"* [12] *He said to them, "Lift me up and hurl me into the sea; then the sea will become quiet for you, for I declare it is on my account that this great storm has come upon you."* [13] *Nevertheless, the men rowed harder than ever to get back to the dry land, but they could not, for the sea grew more and more tempestuous around them.* [14] *Therefore they called out to the LORD, "O LORD, do not let us perish because of this man's life, and do not lay his innocent blood on us. For you, O LORD, have the power to always do what you want."* [15] *So they lifted up Jonah and hurled him into the sea, and at that the sea ceased from its raging.* [16] *Then the men were seized by a great fear of the LORD. And they offered a sacrifice to the LORD and made solemn vows.* [17] *And the LORD appointed a great fish to swallow up Jonah. And Jonah was in the belly of the fish three days and three nights.*

—JONAH 1:11–17

"Hurl Me into the Sea"

Once the sailors learn that Jonah is the cause of the storm, they reason that he is also the key to quieting it. They ask him if there is something that should be done with him, in order to calm the storm. Jonah replies that they should hurl him into the sea. Why does he say this? Is he repenting, and simply saying something like "I deserve death for my sin against God—kill me"? Or are his motives the very opposite? Is he saying something like "I would rather die than obey God and go to Nineveh—kill me"? Is he submitting to God or rebelling against God?

The answer is likely somewhere in the middle. There is no reason to think that Jonah's motives and intentions would be any more orderly and coherent than ours would be in such a moment of peril and crisis. He does not use the language of repentance, nor would it make sense to think that he could turn from rebellion toward submission to God so quickly. As the rest of the book will show, Jonah's journey away from self-righteous pride will be a slow one. On the other hand, if he simply wanted to die rather than go to Assyria, he could have killed himself without going on a voyage. The clue to understanding his outlook at this point is embedded in his answer to their question. Notice that he says nothing about God. His concern is elsewhere. He says that if they throw him into the water, "the sea will become quiet *for you*, for I declare it is on my account that this great storm has come *upon you*." Jonah starts to take responsibility for the situation not because he's looking at God but because he's looking at them. And this is significant.

As we will see, Jonah refused God's mission largely because he did not want to extend mercy to pagans. Yet now he views these terrified men before him. They have been calling on their own gods while he has not spoken to his. They have questioned him respectfully, asking him what they should do, rather than simply killing him. They have done nothing wrong at all. As Leslie Allen writes, the character "of the seaman has evidently banished his nonchalant indifference and touched his conscience."[1]

Jonah may have been moved by nothing higher than pity, but that was far better than contempt. Often the first step in coming to one's senses spiritually is when we finally start thinking of somebody—anybody—other than ourselves. So he is saying something like this: "You are dying for me, but I should be dying for you. I'm the one with whom God is angry. Throw me in."

The sailors continue to act admirably when, despite Jonah's offer, they try to row to shore. Only after they realize that there is no other way to be saved, and only after they acknowledge the gravity of what they are about to do, do they cast Jonah over the side, in fear and trembling and prayer to God.

The Pattern of Substitution

Jonah's pity arouses in him one of the most primordial of human intuitions, namely, that the truest pattern of love is substitutionary. Jonah is saying, "I'll fully take the wrath of the waves so you won't have to." True love meets the needs of the loved one no matter the cost to oneself. All life-changing love is some kind of substitutionary sacrifice.

For a moment think about parenting. Children need you to read, read, and read more to them—and talk, talk, and talk more to them—if they are going to develop the ability to understand and use language. Their intellectual and social skills, and their emotional well-being, are massively shaped by how much time we spend with our children. This entails sacrifice on the part of the parent. We must disrupt our lives for years. Yet if we don't do it, they will grow up with all sorts of problems. It's them or us. We must lose much of our freedom now, or they will not become free, self-sufficient adults later.

There are an infinite number of other examples. Whenever we keep a promise or a vow to someone despite the cost, whenever we forgive someone whom we could pay back, whenever we stay close to a suffering person whose troubles are draining to her and all those around her, we are loving according to the pattern of substitutionary sacrifice. Our loss, whether of money, time, or energy, is their gain. We decrease that they may increase. Yet in such love we are not diminished, but we become stronger, wiser, happier, and deeper. That's the pattern of true love, not a so-called love that uses others to meet our needs for self-realization.

We should not be surprised, then, that when God came into the world in Jesus Christ, he loved us like this. Indeed, we can imagine that the reason that this pattern of love is so transformative in human life is because we are created in God's image, and this is how *he* loves. The example of Jonah points to this.

The Greater Than Jonah

When Jesus speaks of "the sign of Jonah" and calls himself "greater than Jonah" (Matthew 12:41), he means that, as Jonah was sacrificed to save the sailors, so he would die to save us.[2] Of course, the differences between Jonah and Jesus are many and profound. Jonah was cast out for his own sins, but that was not true of Jesus (Hebrews 4:15). Jonah only came near to death and went under the water, while Jesus actually died and came under the weight of our sin and punishment. Yet the similarity is there too. Jacques Ellul writes about the casting of Jonah into the deep:

> *At this point Jonah takes up the role of the scapegoat. The sacrifice he makes saves them. The sea calms down. He saves them humanly and materially. . . . Jonah is an example, e.g. of the Christian way. . . . What counts is that this story is in reality the precise intimation of an infinitely vaster story and one which concerns us directly. What Jonah could not do, but his attitude announces, is done by Jesus Christ. He it is who accepts total condemnation. . . .*
>
> *Jonah is not Jesus Christ . . . but he is one of the long line of types of Jesus, each representing an aspect of what the Son of God will be in totality . . . [and] if it is true that the sacrifice of a man who takes his condemnation can save others around him, then this is far more true when the one sacrificed is the Son of God himself. . . . It is solely because of the sacrifice of Jesus Christ that the sacrifice of Jonah avails and saves.*[3]

Jesus summarizes his mission in Mark 10:45: "For even the Son of Man did not come to be served, but to serve, and to give his life as a ransom for many" (cf. 1 Timothy 1:15, 2:5–6). The word translated "for" in "a ransom for many" is a "preposition of substitution," and so the verse means Jesus died on our behalf.[4] As the hymn says, "Bearing shame and scoffing rude, in my place condemned he stood."[5] When Jesus Christ first came into this world, bearing our humanity, and later went to the cross, bearing our sin, he became the greatest example and fulfillment of the pattern of true love—substitutionary sacrifice.

"The Sea Ceased from Its Raging"

The moment Jonah went under the water, the storm switched off as suddenly as a light being turned off.[6] We are told that the sea "ceased from its raging" (verse 15). Some might see this as poetic personification, a mere rhetorical flourish, but is that all it is? The "anger" of the storm was a real expression of the anger of

God toward his rebellious prophet, which was turned aside when Jonah was cast into the waves. In the same way, Jesus's sacrifice is called a "propitiation" (Romans 3:25; Hebrews 2:17; 1 John 2:2, 4:10), an old word that means Christ dealt with the wrath of God on sin and evil by standing in our place and bearing the punishment we deserve.[7]

Many today find the idea of an angry God to be distasteful, even though modern people agree widely that to be passionate for justice does entail rightful anger.[8] To deny God's wrath upon sin not only robs us of a full view of God's holiness and justice but also can diminish our wonder, love, and praise at what it was that Jesus bore for us. Unlike Jonah, who was being punished only for his own disobedience, Jesus takes the full divine condemnation so there is none left for those who believe (Romans 8:1). He drains the cup of divine justice so there is not a drop left for us (Matthew 26:39,41).

If we read the book of Jonah as a stand-alone text, we could get the impression by this point that the biblical God was ill-tempered and vengeful. But even within the horizon of the entire story, we see that God refrains from giving Jonah all he deserves. Since Jesus is not merely a man but God come to earth, then far from depicting a vindictive deity, the whole Bible shows us a God who comes and bears his own penalty, so great is his mercy.

As we saw previously, Jonah's whole problem was the same as ours: a conviction that if we fully surrender our will to God, he will not be committed to our good and joy. But here is the ultimate proof that this deeply rooted belief is a lie. A God who substitutes himself for us and suffers so that we may go free is a God you can trust.

Jonah mistrusted the goodness of God, but he didn't know about the cross. What is our excuse?

The impact of all this on the pagan sailors is great. When the sea grows perfectly calm, they are "seized" by a greater "fear" than when they thought they would drown. But this is a qualitatively new kind of fear. It is the fear of "the Lord" (verse 16). The sailors use the covenant name "Yahweh," the Hebrew personal name that denotes a personal, saving relationship with him. The fear of the Lord is the essence of all saving knowledge and wisdom (e.g., Psalm 111:10; Proverbs 9:10). The sailors immediately begin to offer oaths and sacrifices to the Lord. They thought of him just as Jonah's tribal deity, but now the deliverance of Jonah helps them see the greatness of who God really is.

Most commentators believe that this means they were converted. Foxhole conversions are notorious. People under duress often make vows to God and offer obeisance when there is impending doom, but after the danger passes, the religious observances and prayers fade away. These men were different. They made their vows after the danger passed. That indicates that they were not seeking God for what he could do for them, but simply for the greatness of who he is in himself. That is the beginning of true faith.

All of this is ironic. Jonah was fleeing God because he did not want to go and show God's truth to wicked pagans, but that is exactly what he ends up doing. Daniel C. Timmer writes: "Jonah's anti-missionary activity has ironically resulted in the conversion of non-Israelites."[9] Another commentator adds: "This carries us farther in the lessons of this book about God's sovereignty. What God is going to do, he will do."[10]

As soon as Jonah hits the water, the God whom he did not trust miraculously saves him. This mysterious divine mercy that Jonah finds so inexplicable and offensive turns out to be his only hope. He does not drown. He is swallowed by a great fish. In that prison, Jonah gets his first insights into the meaning and the wonder of God's grace.

CHAPTER 6

❧

RUNNING FROM GRACE

¹⁷ *And the LORD appointed a great fish to swallow up Jonah. And Jonah was in the belly of the fish three days and three nights.*

¹ *Then Jonah prayed to the LORD his God from the belly of the fish,* ² *saying, "I call out to the LORD, out of my distress, and he answers me; Out of the belly of Sheol I cry, and you hear my voice.* ³ *For you cast me into the deep, into the heart of the seas, and the flood surrounds me; All your waves and your billows pass over me.* ⁴ *Then I said, 'I am driven away from your sight; Nevertheless, I continue to gaze toward your holy temple.'* ⁵ *The waters close in over me to take my life; the abyss surrounds me; weeds are wrapped about my head.* ⁶ *To the roots of the mountains I sink. The netherworld, its bars are closed upon me forever. And yet you lift me up from the pit alive, O LORD my God.* ⁷ *Even when my life ebbs away, I remember the LORD. My prayer comes to you, to the temple of your holiness.* ⁸ *Those clinging to empty idols forfeit the grace that is theirs.* ⁹ *But I, with the voice of thanksgiving will sacrifice to you. What I have vowed I will fulfill. Salvation comes only from the LORD!"* ¹⁰ *And the LORD spoke to the fish, and it vomited Jonah out upon the dry land.*

—JONAH 1:17–2:10

Where Do We Find God's Grace?

The story reveals that God "appointed" a great fish to swallow Jonah. This verb is used several times in the book, as when God appointed a plant to grow and then to die, as we will see in chapter 4 of the book of Jonah. In each case, God orchestrated a circumstance in history to teach Jonah something he desperately needed to know.[1] With 20/20 hindsight, we can see that the most important lessons we have learned in life are the result of God's severe mercies. They are events that were difficult or even excruciating at the time but later came to yield more good in our lives than we could have foreseen.

The great fish is a perfect example of such a severe mercy. Obviously, the fish saved Jonah's life by swallowing him. On the other hand, he was still in a watery prison. He was still sinking to the bottom of the world, to "the roots of the mountains," far from help and hope. He was still alive, but for how long? It was only a temporary respite unless God provided another act of deliverance.

Peter Craigie writes that when we reject and dis-obey God, as Jonah did, it takes "radical treatment, if it [is] to be remedied." He points out that the text has been depicting Jonah as descending—going *down* to Joppa, *down* into a ship, *down* into the depths of the ship—and now, finally, he goes even further *down* into the very depths of the ocean. "But not until he was all the way down, finally stripped of his own buoyant self-sufficiency, was deliverance possible."[2] There was a fatal flaw in Jonah's character, and it had lain hid-den from him as long as his life was going well. It was only through complete failure that he could begin to see it and change it.

This principle works itself out at multiple levels. In J. K. Rowling's Harvard commencement speech in 2008, she described a point in her life in which she had "failed on an epic scale. An exceptionally short-lived marriage had imploded, and I was jobless, a lone parent, and as poor as it is possible to be in modern Britain without being homeless." But, she added, "[I] began to direct all my energy into finishing the only work that mattered to me. Had I really succeeded at anything else, I might never have found the determination to succeed in the one arena, [writing, in which] I believed I truly belonged."[3] In short, she said, her success was built on her failures.

Jacob was not prepared to lead the family of God until he had been forced to flee from his home, experienced years of mistreatment at the hands of his father-in-law, and faced (what he thought was) a violent encounter with is aggrieved brother, Esau. It was only then that Jacob met God face to face (Genesis 32:1–32). Abraham, Joseph, David, Elijah, and Peter all became powerful leaders through failure and suffering. Countless Christians can attest to the same experience. It is only when you reach the very bottom, when everything falls apart, when all your schemes and resources are broken and exhausted, that you are finally open to learning how to completely depend on God. As is often said, you never realize that Jesus is all you need until Jesus is all you have. You must lose your life to find your life (Matthew 10:39).

If Jonah was to begin finally to ascend, both in the water and in faith, he had to be brought to the very end of himself. The way up was, first of all, down. The usual place to learn the greatest secrets of God's grace is at the bottom.

But it is not simply *being* at the bottom that begins to change Jonah but *prayer* at the bottom. As Jack Sasson says, at this point in the story, "the action is about to come to a full halt to leave Jonah alone with his God."[4] Jonah begins to pray, and at the climax of the prayer, he speaks of *chesdh* (Jonah 2:9). It is a key biblical word often translated as "steadfast love" or "grace." It refers to the covenant love of God. It takes the whole prayer for Jonah to get there—to a declaration about God's grace—but when he does, he is released back into the land of the living.

What Is God's Grace?

In his great book *Knowing God*, J. I. Packer observes that many people talk about God's grace, but it is an abstraction to them, not a life-changing power. He goes on to explain that there are several "crucial truths . . .

which the doctrine of grace presupposes, and if they are not acknowledged and felt in one's heart, clear faith in God's grace becomes impossible."[5] Jonah's prayer shows him coming to grips with three of them.

The first truth we must grasp is what Packer calls our "moral ill-desert." That is a hard message for our culture to hear, however. We live in an age marked by "The Triumph of the Therapeutic."[6] We are taught that our problem is a lack of self-esteem, that we live with too much shame and self-incrimination. In addition, we are told, all moral standards are socially constructed and relative, so no one has the right to make you feel guilty. You must determine right or wrong for yourself. In a society dominated by such beliefs, the Bible's persistent message that we are guilty sinners comes across as oppressive if not evil and dangerous. These modern cultural themes make the offer of grace unnecessary, even an insult.

Jonah's prayer, however, recognized that "*you* cast me into the deep, into the heart of the seas" (verse 3). Jonah knew that there was divine justice and that he deserved it.

Second, we must believe in what Packer calls our

"spiritual impotence." We must admit not only our sins but also that we cannot repair or cleanse ourselves from them. Our culture, again, does not help us here, for it is dominated not only by therapy but also by technology. Even if we accept responsibility for wrong-doing, we believe "we can fix this." The most common way we try to do that is to apply the technology of morality. We believe that with hard work and/or fastidious religious observance, we can repair our relationship with God and even put him in a position where he "can't say 'no' to us."[7]

This idea, that we can fix ourselves through moral effort, was certainly around in Jonah's day. It is a foundational assumption of every other religion. But in verse 6, Jonah rightly rejects it. He says he is sinking to "the netherworld," the underwater world farthest from living humanity and God in his temple, and that there "its bars are closed upon me forever." He realizes that he stands condemned and permanently barred for his sin and rebellion, and there is no possible way to open those gates himself or make good his debt. The famous hymn expresses it like this:

Not the labors of my hands
Can fulfill thy law's demands.
Could my zeal no respite know,
Could my tears forever flow,
All for sin could not atone.
Thou must save, and thou alone.[8]

We are "barred" from God, and the doctrine of grace resonates deeply only if we admit we cannot save ourselves.

Amazing Grace

The third truth we must grasp, if we are to understand God's grace in a way that transforms, is how *costly* the salvation is that God provides. Not once but twice in his prayer, Jonah looks not merely toward heaven but "toward your holy temple" (verse 4) and "to the temple of your holiness" (verse 7). Why? Jonah knew that it was over the mercy seat in the temple that God promised to speak to us (Exodus 25:22). The mercy seat was a slab of gold over the top of the Ark of the Covenant, in which resided the tablets of the Ten Commandments. On the Day of Atonement, a priest sprinkled the blood of the atoning sacrifice for the sins of the people on the mercy seat (Leviticus 16:14–15).

What a picture! The temple was the residence of the holy God, his perfect moral righteousness represented by the Ten Commandments, which no human being ever has or ever can keep. How shall we approach God? Won't the law of God condemn us? Yes it would, except for the blood of the atoning sacrifice on the mercy seat, over the Ten Commandments, shielding us from its condemnation. It is only when the death of another secures our forgiveness that we can speak with God.

Neither Jonah nor any other Israelite at that time understood all that this meant, but a better picture of the gospel of Jesus could hardly be imagined. The temple and the sacrificial system established all three of these "grace truths" as a foundation: We are sinners, unable to save ourselves and able to be saved only through extreme and costly measures. Not until centuries later would it be revealed that atonement could not be effected by the blood of bulls and goats but only by the once-for-all sacrifice of Jesus Christ (Hebrews 10:4–10).

J. I. Packer is right. Many people sing "Amazing Grace" and give lip service to the idea, but that grace has not profoundly changed them. God's grace becomes wondrous, endlessly consoling, beautiful, and humbling only when we fully believe, grasp, and remind ourselves of all three of these background truths—that we deserve nothing but condemnation, that we are utterly incapable of saving ourselves, and that God has saved us, despite our sin, at infinite cost to himself. Some people have too high a view of themselves. God's grace is not stunning because they don't feel they need it, or at least, not so much. Others do indeed see themselves as failures but, while they may have some notion of an abstract "God of love," they have little idea of the enormity of Jesus's sacrifice to purchase them out of debt, slavery, and death. They aren't lost in wonder, love, and praise at the lengths and depths to which he has gone for us.

The Shout of Grace

Now we see why we find grace not at the high points of our lives but in the valleys and depths, at the bottom. No human heart will learn its sinfulness and impotence by being told it is sinful. It will have to be *shown*— often in brutal experience. No human heart will dare to believe in such free, costly grace unless it is the only hope. It is a combination of hard circumstances, insight from the biblical gospel of atonement for sin, and prevailing prayer that can move us to wonder and amazement, even in the darkest, deepest places.

Something of this amazement and wonder at grace is hinted at in Jonah's prayer. He has recognized that the "bars are closed upon me forever." However, he immediately adds: *"And yet you lift me up from the pit alive, O Lord"* (verse 6). He is lost, condemned, and unable to unlock the doors of his prison. *And yet* God saves him. Jonah begins to praise God and dedicate himself before he has any assurance that he will escape from the fish by some supernatural deliverance. This is important to notice. It is when he realizes the grace of God that the "great decision is taken."[9] "It is not when history is redirected by some supernatural event . . . that the great miracles occur. It is when a person comes to acknowledge his or her sin and confesses it before God and when, as a consequence, God restores the broken Creator-creature relationship."[10] That's the real deliverance—not the release from the fish.

Jonah's prayer ends with a shout. As he has been piecing together the constituent parts of a doctrine of grace, the wonder of it dawns on him, and in a climactic statement he says, "Salvation comes only from the LORD" (verse 9). Some have called this text the central verse of the Scriptures, or at least, it expresses with great economy of language the main point of the entire Bible.

It says, literally, that salvation is of the Lord, and the prepositional phrase denotes possession.[11] Salvation belongs to God alone, to no one else. If someone is saved, it is wholly God's doing. It is not a matter of God saving you partly and you saving yourself partly. No. God saves us. We do not and cannot save ourselves. That's the gospel.

The Process of Grace

When placed into the context of the entire book of Jonah, however, this prayer has a sobering aspect. In verse 8 Jonah says that "those clinging to empty idols forfeit the grace that is theirs." Jonah rightly says that idolatry blocks people from receiving grace. But what people is he referring to? In the context he is saying that pagans who worship literal statues and idols forfeit the grace of God. While that statement is true, we can't help but read it in light of Jonah's relapse into anger and confusion at God's mercy to the Ninevites, which we will see when we get to chapter 4 of the book of Jonah.

In other words, despite his breakthrough here, Jonah has not grasped grace as deeply as we might at first think he has. There is still a sense of superiority and self-righteousness that will cause him to explode in anger when God has mercy on those Jonah sees as his inferiors. He sees the literal idols that the pagans worship and doesn't see the more subtle idols in his own life that keep him from fully grasping that he too, just like the heathen, lives only, equally by God's grace.

God releases Jonah from the fish even though, as will become obvious soon, his repentance is only partial. Yet the merciful God patiently works with us, flawed and clueless though we are.

CHAPTER 7

DOING JUSTICE, PREACHING WRATH

¹Then the word of the LORD came to Jonah the second time, saying, ² "Arise, go to Nineveh, that great city, and proclaim to her the message that I tell you." ³ So Jonah arose and set out for Nineveh, according to the word of the LORD. Now Nineveh was an exceedingly large city—three days' journey in breadth. ⁴ Jonah went a day's journey into the city and then called out, "In forty days, Nineveh shall be overthrown!" ⁵ And the people of Nineveh believed God. They called for a fast and put on sackcloth, from the greatest of them to the least. ⁶ The word reached the king of Nineveh, and he arose from his throne, stripped off his robe, covered himself with sackcloth, and sat in ashes. ⁷ And he cried out and issued a decree in Nineveh, on the authority of the king and nobles, saying, "By the decree of the king and his nobles: Let no man or beast, no herd or flock, taste anything. Let them not graze or drink water, ⁸ but let man and beast be covered with sackcloth, and let them call out with fervor to God. Let every person forsake his evil way and the violence that he plans toward others. ⁹ Who knows? God may relent and turn from his fierce anger, so that we may not perish."

¹⁰ *When God examined their deeds, how they forsook their evil way, he renounced the disaster he had said he would do to them, and he did not carry it out.*

—JONAH 3:1–10

Why Do People Repent?

Jonah repented, survived in the belly of the fish, washed ashore, and went to Nineveh to preach. He traveled into the city and began to preach: "In forty days, Nineveh shall be overthrown!"

To Jonah's shock, the people neither laughed nor laid hands on him. Instead, the entire city responded. The Hebrew word for "repent" (*shub*—to turn) occurs four times in verses 8–10, and that is the striking, central message of this passage. Against all expectations, the powerful, violent city of Nineveh put on sackcloth—a sign of mass repentance. And they did so "from the greatest of them to the least" (verse 5), from the top to the bottom of the social spectrum. How could this have happened?

Historians have pointed out that about the time of Jonah's mission, Assyria had experienced a series of famines, plagues, revolts, and eclipses, all of which were seen as omens of far worse things to come. Some have argued that this was God's way of preparing the ground for Jonah. "This state of affairs would have made both rulers and subjects unusually attuned to the message of a visiting prophet."[1] So there was some sociological explanation for this response.

While such a movement toward God always has social aspects, since we are embodied beings who live in particular places, cultures, and historical times, nevertheless such factors cannot wholly explain or account for this kind of repentance. Ellul is amazed at what happened. "Nineveh, with its wholly war-like orientation accuses itself of violence (3:8). . . . Nineveh, proud of its power and invincibility, ceases to be itself when it thus humbles itself."[2]

In January of 1907 a revival broke out at a Bible conference in Pyongyang, now the capital of North Korea. Those attending the conference came under deep conviction of sin, especially when a preacher called them to repent of their traditional hatred of the Japanese.[3] Of course, the Korean Christians had accepted the fundamental truths of the gospel of grace, and yet these had not sunk in deeply enough for them to forgive the Japanese. They felt morally superior to a nation they saw as oppressive and cruel. In the light of the gospel, however, the Koreans at the conference saw that they stood before God as equally sinful and condemned with all other human beings, yet rescued by the sheer and costly grace of Christ. This drained away their pride and bitterness.

They returned to their homes with a new willingness to repent of wrongdoing. People went house to house repairing relationships and returning stolen articles. The worship services were filled with a new power.[4] The result was explosive growth of the church. The Methodist church, for example, doubled in membership size in a single year. There have been many such spiritual movements across the world in the history of the church.

How do we explain such phenomena? Many have pointed out that the Japanese-Korean pacts of 1904 and 1907 imposed Japanese rule on the country. Did this sociopolitical background open many Koreans to a Christian message that offered resources for addressing ethnic hatred, for repenting and offering forgiveness? Yes, but can such factors fully explain what happened? Of course not, since these conditions occur constantly in the world and they do not have results such as these.

Repentance is always a work of God (2 Timothy 2:25).

Preaching Justice

However, we must not be too quick to liken Nineveh's "turning" to the revivals of modern church history. While it says they "believed God" (verse 5), there is no indication that the Ninevites came into a covenant relationship with the God of Israel. The word the Ninevites use is "God," the generic word *Elohim*, rather than the personal, covenant name, "Yahweh," that the Lord uses with his people Israel. There is no mention of the residents of Nineveh forsaking their gods and idols. They did not offer sacrifices to the Lord, nor was there any rite of circumcision. This is why almost all commentators agree that Jonah did not successfully convert the Ninevites.[5] What, then, was really happening?

The king of Nineveh understood God to be saying that each citizen of the city must "forsake his evil way and the violence that he plans toward others" (verse 8). *Violence* is "the arbitrary infringement of human rights. . . . Of such social injustice Nineveh was blatantly guilty."[6] Assyrian imperialism, cruelty, and social injustice were condemned by other Hebrew prophets as well (Isaiah 10:13ff; Nahum 3:1,19).

This call to repent of oppression and injustice fits with the messages of other biblical prophets in the relatively few times they spoke to pagan nations. In Amos 1:1–2:3 the prophet denounced Israel's neighbors for their imperialism, cruelty and violence, and oppression of the weak. Biblical scholar Christopher J. H. Wright points out that "in the Old Testament . . . where an Israelite addresses pagan nations, the condemnation is typically targeted at their moral and social wickedness."[7]

That is what Jonah did as well. His message to Nineveh focused on the city's social practices, their "deeds" (verse 10), and the call was to change their ways (verse 4).

As we have seen, the Assyrian empire was unusually violent. It slaughtered and enslaved countless people and oppressed the poor. It was renowned for its injustice, imperialism, and oppression of other countries. Yet the text shows that the impulse toward exploitation and abuse was also eating away at the fabric of Nineveh's society. It wasn't merely that the Assyrians as a nation were oppressing other nations, but individuals were violent toward one another, poisoning social relationships. "Let every person forsake . . . the violence that he plans toward others" (verse 8). The wealthy enslave the poor while the poor strike back through crime, and middle-class people cheat one another. It may be that the repentance "from the greatest of them to the least" (verse 5) shows the beginning of a reconciliation of the various strata of society.

Many argue that while the reported summary of Jonah's message to Nineveh was a bare threat (verse 4), it is reasonable to infer that he gave them more information about God than is mentioned in the text. That is almost certainly true. They did, for example, turn to God in the hope that he would hear them. This makes it likely that at least they questioned Jonah to find out if there was any hope of God's forgiveness.[8]

Nevertheless, the biblical text does not tell us that God sent Jonah with the purpose of converting the populace into a saving, covenant relationship with him. He was warning them about their evil, violent behavior and the inevitable consequences if they did not relent and change.

And while we know from the rest of the Bible that changing social behavior is not sufficient for salvation, and that God cannot give final forgiveness without faith and an atoning sacrifice (cf. Numbers 14:18; Hebrews 9:22), nevertheless, God's response is instructive. Though the people of Nineveh do not forsake their idols and sacrifice to him, God in his mercy relents from his threat to destroy the city. For the time being, he expresses favor in response to the city's intention and effort at social reform.

Preaching God's Wrath

What kind of ministry brought about this remarkable result? Some commentators jump to the conclusion that Jonah preached salvation through faith and the city's response was a great revival. However, as we have seen, there is no evidence of conversion to faith in the Lord. Others conclude that modern-day readers should emulate Jonah by providing social services in cities rather than doing evangelism.[9] However, Jonah did not go to Nineveh just to quietly do social work. He preached the threat of divine judgment loudly in God's name.

What actually happened doesn't fit into either of these categories. There was a coming together of different warring classes and individuals within the body politic in order to bring about social healing and a more just society.[10] And yet it was the result of a preaching ministry that proclaimed the wrath of the biblical God explicitly.

It is hard for us to even imagine today the ministry that happened in Nineveh. Usually those who are most concerned about working for social justice do not also stand up and speak clearly about the God of the Bible's judgment on those who do not do his will. On the other hand, those who publicly preach repentance most forcefully are not usually known for demanding justice for the oppressed.

Nevertheless, this text encourages us to do both. In this instance, God seeks social reform through his prophet, a change in the Ninevites' exploitative and violent behavior. Yet he also directs that the city should be told about a God of wrath who will punish sin. Ellul writes:

> [Jonah] . . . did not become free to select for himself what he would say to men. He did not go to them to tell them about his experiences. . . . He did not decide the content of his preaching. . . . Thus . . . our witness is fast bound to the word of God. The greatest saint or mystic can say nothing of value unless it is based solely on God's word.[11]

We seldom see ministries that are equally committed to preaching the Word fearlessly and to justice and care for the poor, yet these are theologically inseparable. In Isaiah's time Israelite society was marked by greedy exploitation and imperialistic abuses of power, rather than by generous, peaceful service and cooperation. This led to social breakdown and psychological alienation. However, when Isaiah looked at this unjust society he saw "Through the wrath of the Lord of hosts the land is scorched, and the people are like fuel for the fire; no one spares another . . . they devour . . . but are not satisfied. . . . Manasseh devours Ephraim, and Ephraim devours Manasseh . . ." (Isaiah 9:19–21).[12] Isaiah did not see social injustice as merely meriting God's wrath. Rather, the misery and social breakdown, the economic and political "devouring" of one another (yet the inner emptiness and discontent it brings) is all actually the *outworking* of God's wrath.

Imagine if a house were on fire but you couldn't see the flames. As the house crumbled and collapsed, you would wonder what was happening. Only if someone enabled you to see the fire would the dissolution of the building make sense.

Without understanding the wrath of God, it is impossible to fully understand why so many societies, empires, institutions, and lives break down. Referring to this passage in Isaiah, Alec Motyer wrote that in a world created by a good God, evil and injustice are "inherently self-destructive." The resulting social disintegration "expresses [God's] *wrath*. He presides over the cause and effect processes he has built into creation so they are expressions of his holy rule of the world."[13] That is, God has created the world so that cruelty, greed, and exploitation have natural, disintegrative consequences that are a manifestation of his anger toward evil.

To work against social injustice and to call people to repentance before God interlock theologically.

Martin Luther King Jr. did not make the mistake of separating the call for social justice from belief in a God of judgment. In his "Letter from a Birmingham Jail" he responds to the question of how he can advocate civil disobedience, the breaking of some laws, in this case laws of racial segregation. He answered that some laws are unjust.

One has not only a legal but a moral responsibility to obey just laws. Conversely, one has a moral responsibility to disobey unjust laws. I would agree with St. Augustine that "an unjust law is no law at all." Now, what is the difference between the two? How does one determine whether a law is just or unjust? A just law is a man made code that squares with the moral law or the law of God. An unjust law is a code that is out of harmony with the moral law.[14]

Here there is no separation between working for justice in a society and declaring the displeasure of a just God. In his great "I Have a Dream" speech, Dr. King did not appeal to modern, secular individualism. He did not say, "All should be free to define their own meaning in life and moral truth." Rather he quoted Scripture and called his society to "Let [God's] justice roll down like waters, and righteousness like a mighty stream" (Amos 5:24).[15]

The Mystery of Mercy

Even though Jonah let the Ninevites know that forgiveness was possible, that wasn't the main thrust of his preaching. The summary that the text gives us of his sermons was not "In forty days, Nineveh *might* be overthrown" but "In forty days, Nineveh *shall* be overthrown!" That was what Jonah enthusiastically wanted and predicted. He *enjoyed* preaching wrath. He did it with glee, not tears, because he couldn't wait for God's hammer to fall on them.

But God responded with mercy. "When God examined their deeds, how they forsook their evil way, he renounced the disaster he had said he would do to them, and he did not carry it out" (verse 10).

At this, Jonah is plunged back into the depths of his despair and disappointment with God. His response is surprising to the reader, and it sets up the remarkable final chapter of Jonah's encounter with the Lord.

HEART STORMS

¹ *But what God did was so terrible to Jonah, that he burned with anger.* ² *And he prayed to the LORD and said, "O LORD, is this not what I spoke of when I was still in my homeland? That is why I fled with haste to Tarshish; for I knew that you are a gracious and compassionate God, very patient, and abounding in steadfast love, and who also renounces plans for bringing disaster.* ³ *Therefore now, O LORD, please take my life from me, for to me death is better than life."* ⁴ *And the LORD said, "Is it good for you to burn with such anger?"*

—JONAH 4:1–4

Of all the books of the Bible, Jonah has the most un-expected and overlooked final chapter. Most people have heard the story of Jonah, but they think of it as ending at Jonah's repentance and release from the fish.

A smaller number of people may be able to tell you that the story goes on and that Jonah went and preached successfully to Nineveh. Almost everyone thinks the story ends right there. Yet there is a final, startling chapter in which the real lessons of the entire narrative are revealed.

The Incredible Collapse of Jonah

Assyria was the greatest power in the world, and the cruelest. It is understandable that, at first, Jonah did not want to go and preach in its capital. Yet when he finally announced God's coming judgment, there was massive repentance. In response, God granted a reprieve and did not destroy the city.

It was nothing short of astonishing. Many modern readers respond to such a story with skepticism. We are quick to believe accounts of mass violence, but it's harder to believe that the various classes and people of a great city would unite and agree to turn away from injustice. However, that is what happened. It shows that the Word of God is more powerful than we can imagine.

This would lead us to expect that the book would end in chapter 3 on a note of triumph, with "and Jonah returned to his own land rejoicing." Instead, events take an unexpected turn. "But what God did was so terrible to Jonah, that he burned with anger" (verse 1). The reaction is shocking and inexplicable. Do artists get angry when a prominent museum accepts their art for an installation? Do musicians get angry when they are given a standing ovation at Carnegie Hall? Why, then, when Jonah has just preached to the toughest audience of his life—and they have responded positively down to the last person—would he melt down in furious rage?

The Theological Problem

What specifically was Jonah's problem?

In verse 2 he says, "Oh Lord, is this not what I spoke of when I was still in my homeland?" Readers are now let in on the ongoing argument Jonah has been having with God all along. Verses 2 and 3 give us a brief sample, but it is not hard to imagine the rest of it. "I just *knew* you might do something like this! These people are *evil*, and they only changed because they were scared. They didn't convert and start worshipping you. They merely promised to start changing—and you bestow mercy on them for that! It's good that you are a God of mercy, but this time you've gone too far."

The name "Yahweh" (translated "the Lord") has not appeared since chapter 2, but now Jonah literally cries, "Alas, Yahweh!" This is the personal, covenant name of God, which he reveals only to his people Israel, and it is the covenant of God with Israel that is much in Jonah's mind. The Lord had promised to preserve Israel and accomplish his purposes in the world through them. How can God keep his promises to uphold his people and at the same time show mercy to his people's enemies? How can he claim to be a God of justice and allow such evil and violence to go unpunished?

In Jonah's mind, then, the issue is a theological one. There seems to be a contradiction between the justice of God and the love of God. "He knew that God loved Israel and extended his mercy to his chosen people; he felt, in the very marrow of his bones, that this special love of God . . . should not be extended to gentiles, above all to evil gentiles such as the inhabitants of Nineveh."[1]

The Heart Issue

Jonah's great anger, however, shows that he was not merely perplexed by a theological conundrum. When he says he wants to die (verse 3) and God, with remarkable gentleness, chastises him for his inordinate anger (verse 4), we see that Jonah's real problem was at the deepest level of his heart. Perhaps we could say that all theological problems play themselves out not merely in our intellects but in our commitments, desires, and identities.

When Jonah says, in effect, "Without that—I have

no desire to go on," he means he has lost something that had replaced God as the main joy, reason, and love of his life. He had a relationship with God, but there was something else he valued more. His explosive anger shows that he is willing to discard his relationship with God if he does not get this thing. When you say, "I won't serve you, God, if you don't give me X," then X is your true bottom line, your highest love, your real god, the thing you most trust and rest in. Here is Jonah saying to God, who should be the only real source of his meaning in life, "I have no source of meaning!"

What was it for Jonah? Nineveh's repentance was pleasing to God, but it was threatening to Israel's national interests. The will of God and the political fortunes of Israel seemed to be diverging. One would have to be chosen, and Jonah leaves no doubt as to which of those two concerns was more important to him. Of course, anyone who cared for his own country would have been anxious about Assyria's survival. It was a terrorist state. Jonah, however, did not turn to

God with his anxiety, trusting in him as so many of the psalm writers had done. If he had to choose between the security of Israel and loyalty to God, well, he was ready to push God away. That is not just concern and love for one's country; that is a kind of deification of it.

Some years ago I was preaching on this passage in Jonah, and after the sermon a listener expressed his displeasure. He did not feel I should have criticized Jonah. "Jonah was just a good patriot," he told me. "We should all be patriots." I answered him that while love of country and your people is a good thing, like any other love, it can become inordinate. If love for your country's interests leads you to exploit people or, in this case, to root for an entire class of people to be spiritually lost, then you love your nation more than God. That is idolatry, by any definition.

As a missionary, Jonah should have been glad that the Ninevites had taken a first step. Coming to full faith in God does not usually happen overnight, as it did with the sailors in Jonah's boat. The people of the city showed their willingness to repent, and Jonah should have prepared to help them continue in their journey by teaching them the character of this new God, the Lord, and what it means to be in a covenant relationship with him. Instead he was furious that they had even begun to move toward God. Rather than going back into the city to teach and preach, he stayed outside it, in hopes that maybe God would still judge it (Jonah 4:5).

When Christian believers care more for their own interests and security than for the good and salvation of other races and ethnicities, they are sinning like Jonah. If they value the economic and military flourishing of their country over the good of the human race and the furtherance of God's work in the world, they are sinning like Jonah. Their identity is more rooted in their race and nationality than in being saved sinners and children of God. Jonah's rightful love for his country and people had become inordinate, too great, rivaling God. Rightful racial pride can become racism. Rightful national pride and patriotism can become imperialism.

Misusing the Bible

When Jonah begins to berate God, he quotes God's own words to him. They are from Exodus 34:6–7, where God reveals himself to Moses and says he is "compassionate and gracious" and that he "forgives wickedness." "Jonah sets God against God . . . all to justify himself."[2] He reads the Bible selectively, ignoring the latter part of Exodus 34:7 that speaks of God not leaving "the guilty unpunished." He creates a simplistic picture of a God who simply loves everyone without judgment on evil. He uses the sacred text to justify his inordinate indignation, anger, and bitterness.

What Jonah is doing is a great danger for religious people, even the most devout Christians. It is possible to use the Bible selectively to justify oneself.[3] One example is the scholar who "dissects Scripture to set it against Scripture" in a way that undermines the Bible's authority so we don't have to obey it. Another is "the simple Christian who opens his Bible to find himself justified . . . against non-Christians or Christians who do not hold the same views, arguments which show how far superior my position is to that of others."[4] Whenever we read the Bible in order to say, "Aha! I'm right!"; whenever we read it to feel righteous and wise in our own eyes, we are using the Bible to make ourselves into fools or worse, since the Bible says that the mark of evil fools is to be "wise in their own eyes" (cf. Proverbs 26:12).

In other words, if we feel more righteous as we read the Bible, we are misreading it; we are missing its central message. We are reading and using the Bible rightly only when it humbles us, critiques us, and encourages us with God's love and grace despite our flaws.

> For what [the Bible] teaches us about ourselves is all to the effect that we are not righteous, that we have no means of justifying ourselves, that we have . . . no right to condemn others and be in the right against them, and that . . . only a gracious act of God . . . can save us. That is what Scripture teaches us, and if we stick to this, reading the Bible is useful and healthy and brings forth fruit in us.[5]

Ellul concludes that if we use the Bible to puff up our own egos with our correctness and righteousness, and to denounce all others, then studying the Scripture "becomes a source of death and Satan's work."[6] The one other example we have of anyone quoting and twisting the Bible to resist God is when Satan does it against Jesus in the wilderness (Matthew 4:1–11). Indeed, Jonah's use of the Bible is not bringing him joy but rather taking him to the brink of despair. He asks God to take away his life.

The Problem of Self-righteousness

In hindsight, there was a clue to Jonah's future meltdown within his prayer in the great fish.

Jonah had fled in the first place because he thought God was going to be merciful to Israel's enemies and therefore, in his view, unjust. Then in chapter 2 he was confronted with the reality that *he* needed mercy and had no hope if God was completely fair with him and gave him only what he deserved. Therefore, in the belly of the fish Jonah received a deeper understanding of his need for grace.

However, at the very end of his prayer he said that those who cling to idols forfeit God's love (Jonah 2:8). Jonah had seen some of his need for grace, but there was still some pride left. Pagans have idols—but not him! Yes, of course he needed mercy, but surely he wasn't on the same level as these people. Surely he still had some spiritual merit—he still had *some* claims on God. The social psychologist Jonathan Haidt concludes from his research that "self-righteousness is the normal human condition."[7] That fits in with what the Bible says about the inevitable human desire to justify oneself through one's performance and effort, and therefore to "boast" in one's righteousness, race and pedigree, or accomplishments (cf. Jeremiah 9:23–26; Romans 3:27–31).

Jonah's self-righteousness had been diminished somewhat but not destroyed. He cried, "Salvation comes only from the LORD!" yet also, in effect, "But I'm not like those awful pagans!" (Jonah 2:8–9). That is why he was still susceptible to the spiritual crash that happened to him after God showed Nineveh mercy. He still felt, to some degree, that mercy had to be deserved, and they didn't deserve it.

We learn from Jonah that understanding God's grace—and being changed by it—always requires a long journey with successive stages. It cannot happen in a single cathartic or catastrophic experience (like being swallowed by a fish!).

During the building of Interstate 79 from Pittsburgh to Lake Erie, one stretch remained unfinished for years because of a swamp that had to be crossed. They kept putting down pilings, trying to finally get to the bottom so the bridge would not sink. But whenever they thought they had gotten to bedrock, the piling would give way and they would have to drill deeper.

Jonah's heart was like that. Every time it seemed he had taken God and his grace to the very bottom, it turned out that he needed to go deeper. What does it mean to get to "bedrock" in one's heart? If you say, "I'll obey you, Lord, *if* you give me that," then "that" is the nonnegotiable and God is just a means to an end. "That"—whatever it is—is the real bedrock. It is more foundational to your happiness than God is.

As long as there is something more important than God to your heart, you will be, like Jonah, both fragile and self-righteous. Whatever it is, it will create pride and an inclination to look down upon those who do not have it. It will also create fear and insecurity. It is the basis for your happiness, and if anything threatens it, you will be overwhelmed with anger, anxiety, and despair.

To reach heart bedrock with God's grace is to recognize all the ways that we make good things into idols and ways of saving ourselves. It is to instead finally recognize that we live wholly by God's grace. Then we begin serving the Lord not in order to get things from him but just for *him*, for his own sake, just for who he is, for the joy of knowing him, delighting him, and becoming like him. When we've reached bedrock with God's grace, it begins to drain us, slowly but surely, of both self-righteousness and fear.

God quietly rebukes Jonah with a question: "Is it good for you to burn with such anger?" (Jonah 4:4). Anger is not wrong. If you love something and it is threatened or harmed, anger is the proper response. But "such" anger—inordinate anger of self-righteousness and fear—is a sign that the thing Jonah loves is a counterfeit god. He is inordinately committed to his race and nation. God will have to deal with this idolatry if Jonah is ever to get the infinite peace of resting in God's grace alone.

CHAPTER 9

༂ཉ

THE CHARACTER
OF COMPASSION

⁴ And the LORD said, "Is it good for you to burn with such anger?" ⁵ Jonah then left the city and sat down just east of it and made a shelter for himself there. He sat under it in the shade, waiting to see what would happen to the city. ⁶ To deliver him from his dejection, the LORD God appointed a plant that grew rapidly up over Jonah, to be a shade over his head. And Jonah was delighted and glad for the plant. ⁷ But at the break of dawn the next day, God appointed a worm that attacked the plant, so that it withered. ⁸ And when the sun rose higher, God appointed a cutting east wind, and the sun beat down on the head of Jonah so that he was faint and weak. And he longed to die, thinking, "It is better for me to die than to live." ⁹ But God said to Jonah, "Is it good for you to be so angry and dejected over the plant?" And he said, "Yes, it is. I am angry and dejected enough to die." ¹⁰ And the LORD said, "You had compassion for the plant, which you did not plant, you did not make grow, and which came into being and perished in one night. ¹¹ And should I not have compassion for Nineveh, that great city, in which there are more than

120,000 persons who do not know their right hand from their left, and so much livestock?"

—JONAH 4:4–11

The God Who Is Patient

Jonah seemingly had a conversion experience in the fish. He grasped God's grace and obeyed the command to preach God's Word fearlessly. He predicted that the wrath of God was about to fall—but then nothing happened. He felt like a fool. They deserved God's judgment. So why extend mercy to them? The wrath of God had earlier come upon Jonah in that lethal storm, and he had survived only because of the mercy of God. He too had deserved judgment, received mercy instead, and been glad for it. Now all that is forgotten. Jonah is like the ungrateful servant who, having been forgiven, refuses to forgive others (Matthew 18:21–35).

Despite all this, God is patient with him. Jonah

returns to the same angry opposition to God he had at the outset. This time, however, God does not send a towering storm but instead begins to counsel Jonah gently. He asks him the kind of question a therapist might pose: "Is it good for you to burn with such anger?" (Jonah 4:4).

This is both a lesson in humility and a strong consolation. Often we give people the impression that "after conversion every thing is rosy, there are no more problems, one is automatically in tune with God's will. . . . It is not hard but sweet to do what God demands." On the contrary, "Paul speaks of two men battling in him [the 'old man' and the 'new man'] Jonah shows it too. . . . We continue to be sinners" (cf. Galatians 5:17; Ephesians 4:22–24). Of course, we cannot use this to justify bad behavior, but we can take the deepest comfort in seeing that "God knows the totality of [the human heart] . . . that this does not exhaust God's love and patience, that he continues to take this rebellious child by the hand."[1]

The God Who Weeps

God comes to Jonah one more time and begins to reason with him. What is his strategy with his depressed, spiritually blind prophet?

Jonah still has a great deal of self-righteousness. His response to God's mercy foreshadows that of the elder brother in Jesus's parable in Luke 15. When he sees God begin to have mercy on sinners, he is offended. There is an angry exchange with God in 4:1–5. After that, Jonah decides to stay near the city, making himself a temporary shelter. Even though God declared a stay of execution, Jonah still wants to see "what would happen to the city," meaning he still had hopes that God would not spare Nineveh for a long period of time.[2]

To make Jonah's stay more comfortable, God directs a *gigayon*—a shade plant—to grow up. Commentators have identified this as the *Ricinus* or castor oil plant, which grows very quickly and provides shade with its broad leaves.[3] We are told that Jonah is "delighted and glad," unusually strong words. In deep

116

discouragement and grief, sometimes rather small comforts can be particularly sustaining. Self-pity may have played a role in his joy over the plant. "Well, finally," Jonah may have said to himself, "something is going right for me."

Jonah is therefore all the more shocked and angry when God sends a worm to gnaw and wither the plant just as a season of brutally hot, windy weather is beginning. "Unbelievable!" we can imagine him saying. "On top of everything else—this?! Why can't I ever catch a break with God?" Jonah's anger is renewed along with his despair. "I am angry and dejected enough to die," he says (Jonah 4:9). Yet all this has been preparation for God's next assault on Jonah's self-righteousness. This last divine speech to Jonah is brief but sharp and logical.

Ancient philosophers spoke of "the love of benevolence." This meant doing good and helpful things for people even if you didn't like them. It was an exercise of the will. It meant performing loving actions even if your heart was not drawn out in affection for someone. In contrast there was the "love of attachment" in which you loved someone because your heart was bound up with them in attraction and loving desire. The Greek Stoic philosophers insisted that God was marked by *apatheia*. God could certainly do loving things, but a god could not have heart attachment to mere human beings.[4] That is why God's language here is shocking.

The word used in verses 10 and 11 for "compassion" is a word that means to grieve over someone or something, to have your heart broken, to weep for it.[5] God says, "You had compassion for the plant" (verse 10). That is, God says, "You wept over it, Jonah. Your heart became attached to it. When it died, it grieved you." Then God says, in essence, "You weep over plants, but my compassion is for people."

For God to apply this word to himself is radical. This is the language of attachment. God weeps over the evil and lostness of Nineveh. When you put your love on someone, you can be happy only if they are happy, and their distress becomes your distress. The love of attachment makes you vulnerable to suffering, and yet that is what God says about himself—here and in other places (cf. Isaiah 63:9). In Genesis 6:6 it says that when God looked down on the evil of the earth, "his heart was filled with pain."[6] While this language cannot mean that the eternal, unchangeable God loses any of his omnipotence or sovereignty, it is a strong declaration at which we must marvel.[7]

Most of our deepest attachments as human beings are involuntary. Jonah did not look at the *Ricinus* plant and say, "I'm going to attach my heart to you in affection." We need many things, and we get emotionally attached to things that meet those needs. God, however, needs nothing. He is utterly and perfectly happy in himself, and he doesn't need us. So how could he get attached to us?

The only answer is that an infinite, omnipotent, self-sufficient divine being loves only voluntarily. The whole universe is no bigger to God than a piece of lint is to us, and we are smaller pieces of lint on the lint. How could God be attached to us? How could God say, "What happens to Nineveh affects me. It moves me. It grieves me"? It means he voluntarily attaches his heart. Elsewhere we see God looking at Israel, sinking into evil and sin, and God speaks about his heart literally turning over within him. "How can I give you up, O Ephraim? How can I hand you over, O Israel? . . . My heart recoils within me; my compassion grows warm and tender" (Hosea 11:8, ESV).

The God Who Is Generous

God's compassion is not something abstract but concrete. It plays out not just in his attitude but in his actions toward human beings. It is intriguing that he speaks of these violent, sinful pagans as people "who do not know their right hand from their left" (Jonah 4:11). That is an exceedingly generous way to look at Nineveh! It's a figure of speech that means they are spiritually blind, they have lost their way, and they haven't the first clue as to the source of their problems or what to do about them. Obviously, God's threat to destroy Nineveh shows that this blindness and ignorance is ultimately no excuse for the evil they have done, but it shows remarkable sympathy and understanding.

There are many people who have no idea what they should be living for, or the meaning of their lives, nor have they any guide to tell right from wrong. God looks down at people in that kind of spiritual fog, that spiritual stupidity, and he doesn't say, "You idiots." When we look at people who have brought trouble into their lives by their own foolishness, we say things like "Serves them right" or we mock them on social media: "What kind of imbecile says something like this?" When we see people of the other political party defeated, we just gloat. This is all a way of detaching ourselves from them. We distance ourselves from them partly out of pride and partly because we don't want their unhappiness to be ours. God doesn't do that. Real compassion, the voluntary attachment of our heart to others, means the sadness of their condition makes us sad; it affects us. That is deeply uncomfortable, but it is the character of compassion.

God's evident generosity of spirit toward the city could not be a greater indictment of Jonah's ungenerous narrowness, what John Calvin calls his greatest sin, namely that he was "very inhuman" in his attitude toward Nineveh.[8]

"They Don't Know What They Are Doing"

If you are acquainted at all with the New Testament, it is impossible to read about this generous God without remembering Jesus. God is saying to Jonah, "I am weeping and grieving over this city—why aren't you? If you are my prophet, why don't you have my compassion?" Jonah did not weep over the city, but Jesus, the true prophet, did.

Jesus was riding into Jerusalem on the last week of his life. He knew he would suffer at the hands of the leaders and the mob of this city, but instead of being full of wrath or absorbed with self-pity, like Jonah, when he "saw the city, he wept over it and said, 'If you, even you, had only known on this day what would bring you peace—but now it is hidden from your eyes . . . because you did not recognize the time of

God's coming to you" (Luke 19:41–42,44). "Jerusalem, Jerusalem . . . how often I have longed to gather your children together, as a hen gathers her chicks under her wings, and you were not willing" (Luke 13:34).

On the cross, Jesus cried out, "Father, forgive them, for they do not know what they are doing" (Luke 23:34). Jesus is saying, "Father, they are torturing and killing me. They are denying and betraying me. But none of them, not even the Pharisees, really completely understand what they are doing." We can only look in wonder on such a heart. He does not say they are not guilty of wrongdoing. They are—that is why they need forgiveness. Yet Jesus is also remembering that they are confused, somewhat clueless, and not really able to recognize the horror of what they are doing. Here is a perfect heart—perfect in generous love— not excusing, not harshly condemning. He is the weeping God of Jonah 4 in human form.

Over a century ago the great Princeton theologian B. B. Warfield wrote a remarkable scholarly essay called "The Emotional Life of Our Lord," where he considered every recorded instance in the gospels that described the emotions of Christ. He concluded that by far the most typical statement of Jesus's emotional life was the phrase "he was moved with compassion," a Greek phrase that literally means he was moved from the depths of his being.[9] The Bible records Jesus Christ weeping twenty times for every one time it notes that he laughs. He was a man of sorrows, and not because he was naturally depressive. No, he had enormous joy in the Holy Spirit and in his Father (cf. Luke 10:21), and yet he grieved far more than he laughed because his compassion connected him with us. Our sadness makes him sad; our pain brings him pain.

Jesus is the prophet Jonah should have been. Yet, of course, he is infinitely more than that. Jesus did not merely weep for us; he died for us. Jonah went outside the city, hoping to witness its condemnation, but Jesus Christ went outside the city to die on a cross to accomplish its salvation.

Here God says he is grieving over Nineveh, which means he is letting the evil of the city weigh on him. In some mysterious sense, he is suffering because of its sin. When God came into the world in Jesus Christ and went to the cross, however, he didn't experience only emotional pain but every kind of pain in unimaginable dimensions. The agonizing physical pain of the crucifixion included torture, slow suffocation, and excruciating death. Even beyond that, when Jesus hung on the cross, he underwent the infinite and most unfathomable pain of all—separation from God and all love, eternal alienation, the wages of sin. He did it all for us, out of his unimaginable compassion.

"God Is a Complex Character"

This brings us back to the theological problem of Jonah.

How can God relent from judging evildoers? How can he forgive and not punish sin? Many people in the modern West are not troubled by God's mercy because they don't accept the idea of a God who judges. They want a "God of love," but a God who does not get angry when evil destroys the creation he loves is ultimately not a loving God at all. If you love some-one, you must and will get angry if something threat-ens to destroy him or her. As some have pointed out, you have to have had a pretty comfortable life—without any experience of oppression and injustice yourself—to not want a God who punishes sin. One writer, who had seen genocide in his homeland, wrote that "it takes the quiet of a suburban home for the birth of the thesis" that we should desire a "God who refuses to judge." He adds that "in a sun-scorched land, soaked in the blood of the innocent," such an idea "will invariably die."[10]

So God, if he is God, must punish evil. Then how can he also be merciful? How can a holy and righteous God forgive those who deserve divine retribution? How can God be perfectly holy and yet completely loving at the same time?

Many share Jonah's difficulty. Some years ago I was in a study of the book of Jonah with a woman who had very little religious background. When we were done, the woman, who was an art critic and skilled at read-ing literature, sat back and simply marveled. She said that she had always thought of the Bible as basically marked by melodrama. Melodramatic stories have one-dimensional characters that are either all good or all evil. She went on, "And I thought the God of the Bible was just a figure of melodrama, smiting the pagans and blessing believers," she said. "But the God of this book is not like that at all. He is an extremely *complex* character. He sometimes blesses believers and judges the pagans, but at other times he blesses the pagans and punishes the believers. He's not just a being of wrath or love—he's both, and in unpredictable ways." How can he be both at the same time?[11]

In Exodus 33:18 Moses asks to see God's glory. God replies that to see his glory would be fatal, but he offers to shelter him in the cleft of a rock, to let "all my goodness" pass before Moses, though he will see only "my back" (Exodus 33:23). Then, when God shows himself to Moses in 34:6–7, and all God's goodness passes before him, Moses hears God put his goodness into verbal form. He says he is "compassion-ate and gracious . . . forgiving wickedness, rebellion and sin" but then adds, "yet he does not leave the guilty unpunished." Remember Jonah's accusation using God's own words from Exodus 34? This second statement is the part of God's declaration to Moses that Jonah wrongly left out. God said to Moses that he is *both* compassionate *and* committed to punishing evil. These are both aspects of his goodness that God declares. He says, "Here is *all* my goodness. I'm infinitely loving and I want to pardon everybody, and I'm infinitely just and I never let sin go unpunished."

It seems like a striking contradiction, but upon reflection it can be seen that the single word "goodness" binds these apparently contradictory traits together. Why is it that God must punish sin? It's because he would not be perfectly good if he overlooked evil. But then why does God not want people to be lost? Because he's too good, in the sense of being loving. He would not be perfectly good if he just let everyone perish. So his righteousness and his love, far from being at loggerheads, are both simply functions of his goodness. He could not be infinitely and perfectly good unless he was endlessly loving and perfectly just.

Nevertheless, we still experience a contradiction. We don't see *how* he can both punish sin *and* accept and forgive sinners. We reason: Either God is perfectly just, and then will only love people who obey all the commandments, or he's perfectly loving, and will overlook a lot of sin that really should be punished. We think God could not be *all* good in being perfectly just and perfectly loving at once. If we lived at the same point in redemptive history as Moses or Jonah, we would, like them, see no real way forward. Moses saw only the "back parts" of his goodness. It remained a mystery to him, as it was to Jonah.

But we don't stand where they stood.

In John 1, the gospel writer has the audacity to say, "Jesus Christ became flesh and [literally] *tabernacled* among us" (John 1:14). Using this term deliberately evokes the story of Moses, since God's glory dwelt in the tabernacle. Paul likewise says that we see "the light of the knowledge of God's glory displayed in the face of Christ" and that it is "the light of the gospel that displays the glory of Christ" (2 Corinthians 4:4,6).

Through Jesus Christ, and only through him, we can see *all* the goodness of God that Moses wasn't allowed to see and that Jonah couldn't discern. If Jesus Christ died on the cross for our sins, that's how God can be infinitely just, because all sin was punished there, and it's how God can be infinitely loving, because he took it onto himself.

If you don't believe in the gospel of Jesus Christ, you might believe in a God who just accepts everyone no matter how they live or behave. That might be a bit comforting, but is it electrifying and glorious? Or you could have a God who's only just, and the sole way you can get to heaven is if you live an exceptionally good life. That might be bracing, but is that beautiful? Does it move you and change your heart?

Only when you look into the gospel of Jesus Christ does all the goodness of God pass before you, and it's not the back parts anymore. Now you know how he did it. There's the glory of God in the face of Christ through the gospel.[12]

The Goodness and Severity of God

On the cross the justice of God exacted full punishment for sin and in the same moment provided a free salvation to all who believe. On the cross both the justice and love of God fully cooperate, have their way, and shine out brilliantly. "God presented Christ as a sacrifice of atonement, through the shedding of his blood—to be received by faith . . . so as to be just and the one who justifies those who have faith in Jesus" (Romans 3:25–26). As Martin Luther put it, when a Christian believes, he or she is *simul justus et peccator*—simultaneously righteous in God's sight and yet still a sinner.

Even though Jonah never receives an answer to his question about how God can be simultaneously gracious and just, Jonah's story exhibits both the goodness and the severity of God in living color. On the one hand, Jonah receives grace upon grace. Perhaps no other Old Testament prophet looks as bad as Jonah. Jeremiah and Habakkuk often struggled with the messages God gave them to convey to the people. However, Jonah literally ran away from the Lord rather than declare his Word.

Elijah became desperate enough to ask for death (1 Kings 19:4), but that was because the people had failed to believe his preaching. Jonah also asks for death (Jonah 4:3), but it is *because* the people believe him. At every point in the story, Jonah falls lower in the test not only than other prophets before him but also than the supposedly benighted, profane pagans around him. Yet God continues to save him, be patient with him, work with him.

Nevertheless, God does not just accept Jonah and leave him alone. He does not allow Jonah to remain undisturbed in his foolish, wrongful attitudes and behavior patterns. God sends a storm, a fish, a plant. He commissions him again and again and in the end counsels and debates with him directly. Here we see God's righteousness and love working together. He is both too holy and too loving to either destroy Jonah or to allow Jonah to remain as he is, and God is also too holy and too loving to allow us to remain as we are.

The book of Jonah, then, indeed shows us that God is often a confusing, complex character. This is not to deny the historical Christian doctrine of the "simplicity" of God, namely, that God is not a composition of "parts" but rather that all the attributes of God are ultimately one with one another. God does not have a "love" part and a "righteousness" part that must be reconciled. What we see as being in tension is ultimately a perfect unity.

However, that unity can be seen only in light of the work of Jesus Christ. To be confused or angry at God is quite natural. But if we remain in that condition, as Jonah did, it will be because we do not embrace the gospel of salvation through faith in Christ alone, the gospel of which Jonah himself was a sign.

The Cliff-hanger

One of the most notable features of the book of Jonah is its surprising "cliff-hanger" ending. The entire story has been one of God pursuing Jonah, first with a fearsome storm, then with gentle questions and reasoning. Yet even though the methods vary, the purpose remains the same. God wants Jonah to see himself, to recognize the ways that he continues to deny God's grace and the ways he holds on to self-righteousness. He poses one final question: "You don't want me to have compassion on Nineveh, but shouldn't I? In light of all I've shown you, Jonah— should I not love this city, and should you not join me?"

Without an answer, the book ends! We are never told what Jonah's response was, whether he understood and accepted the logic of God's mercy.

We feel that there must be a missing page. Why would the story end so abruptly? One commentator, like many others, suggests: "[The book] forces us to contemplate our personal destiny. It remains unfinished in order that we may provide our own conclusion. . . . For you are Jonah; I am Jonah."[13] It is as if God shoots this arrow of a question at Jonah, but Jonah disappears, and we realize that the arrow is aimed at us. How will you answer?

Because the book of Jonah ends this way, the text

invites us to write our own final paragraphs and chapters. That is, God calls us to apply this text to our own lives, in our own time and place. The introduction showed three layers to the Jonah story—Jonah and God's Word, Jonah in God's world, and Jonah and God's grace. So what is *our* relationship to God's Word, world, and grace? In the next chapters we consider all the episodes in the life of Jonah and ask—what does that mean for us today?

CHAPTER 10

OUR RELATIONSHIP TO GOD'S WORD

Running from God (Jonah 1:1–3)

God commanded Jonah to go to Nineveh, but he ran in the very opposite direction. Why did he do it? We have seen that at the root of Jonah's disobedience was his mistrust in the goodness of God. He did not believe God had his best interests at heart.

If you want to understand your own behavior, you must understand that all sin against God is grounded in a refusal to believe that God is more dedicated to our good, and more aware of what that is, than we are. We distrust God because we assume he is not truly for us, that if we give him complete control, we will be miserable.

Adam and Eve did not say, "Let's be evil. Let's ruin our own lives and everyone else's too!" Rather they thought, "We just want to be happy. But his commands don't look like they will give us the things that we need to thrive. We will have to take things into our own hands—we can't trust him." Jonah is doing the same thing. He is recapitulating the history of the human race and showing us how our own hearts operate every single day. Seldom do human beings lie, twist the truth, cheat, exploit, manipulate, act selfishly, break promises, destroy relationships, or burn with resentment motivated by a simple desire to be evil.

Although we may have been taught that we shouldn't lie or be unfaithful to our spouses, people find themselves at a crossroads where they say, "If I obey God I'll miss out! I need to be happy." That's the justification. Sin always begins with the character assassination of God. We believe that God has put us in a world of delights but has determined that he will not give them to us if we obey him. This is the lie of the serpent, the original temptation of Satan to Adam and Eve that brought about the Fall (Genesis 3:4–5). The serpent told the human race that disobeying God was the only way to realize their fullest happiness and potential, and this delusion has sunk deep into every human heart.[1]

One of the main reasons that we trust God too little is because we trust our own wisdom too much. We think we know far better than God how our lives should go and what will make us happy. Every human being who has lived into middle age knows how often we have been mistaken about that. Yet our hearts continue to operate on this same principle, year after year. We remember how foolish we were at age twenty but think now that we are forty we *know*. But only God knows.

Therefore, because of our deep mistrust of God's goodness and Word, we do everything we can to get out from under his hand. This is really the most fundamental temptation that there has ever been in the world, and the original sin. Specific details may vary, but the deep heart song of "I have to look out for myself" is always there.

Jonah mistrusted God and ran from him. What should he have done instead?

Years earlier, God had given Abraham a command that made absolutely no sense. "Take your son, your only son, whom you love. . . . Sacrifice him . . . as a burnt offering on a mountain I will show you" (Genesis 22:2). No reasons were given, and God had never before asked for human sacrifice—it was an abomination. Also, he had promised in a solemn covenant to make Abraham's descendants more numerous than the sand. God's Word to Abraham was even more inexplicable than his Word to Jonah. Nevertheless, what did Abraham do? He went up the mountain. He refused to act as if he knew best. He reminded himself who God was. Abraham himself had said earlier, "Will not the Judge of all the earth do right?" (Genesis 18:25). From our vantage point today we can see many things that God was doing in Abraham's life. He did not know then that God was strengthening his faith, but he didn't need to. He trusted God.

Jonah knew the story of Abraham and of his faith. That should have been a spiritual resource for him.

He could have followed in Abraham's footsteps, but he did not. We have even less excuse than Jonah, because we have an infinitely greater resource in Jesus Christ. He saved us by saying, under unimaginable pressure, "Nevertheless, not as I will, but as thou wilt" (Matthew 26:39).[2]

The mission God gave Jonah meant possible death and suffering. This is a call that many Christians have heard over the years, going to preach and do good in parts of the world where sudden death is possible every day.[3] Jonah, however, refused to go, thinking only of himself. The mission God gave Jesus, however, meant *certain* death and infinite suffering, and yet he went, thinking not of himself but of us. The "cup" of which Jesus spoke referred to Christ's bearing in our place the divine wrath on sin, our penalty.

And if you see him doing that for you, and if you take the wonder of it deep into your heart, it will finally kill off that stubborn belief that you can't trust God's goodness. You can begin to say, "He *is* good! If he did all that for me, he must love me. He must be willing to do anything to give me joy and what I need." If you see Jesus trusting God in the dark in order to save us, we will be able to trust him when things are confusing and difficult.

The World's Storms (Jonah 1:3–4)

Jonah ran from God, but a storm pursued him. Whenever we disobey God, we are violating our own design, since God created us to serve, know, and enjoy him. There are natural consequences, and so, as it were, all sin has a storm attached to it. Yet we see that the storm not only came upon Jonah, who deserved it, but also upon the sailors in the boat with him, who did not. Life in the world is filled with storms—with difficulties and suffering—some of which we have directly brought on ourselves but many of which we have not.

In either case, God can work out his good purposes in our lives through the storms that come upon us (Romans 8:28).

One reason for storms in our lives is to get us to depend on God and discover his love and strength in ways we would never do otherwise. In a pastoral letter on trials and temptations, the Anglican minister John Newton wrote that it is only when we are in the most pain that God's "power, wisdom, and grace in supporting the soul" may become evident, enabling it to hold up and even triumph "under such pressures as are evidently beyond its own strength to sustain."[4] Another way God works through suffering, Newton writes, is that suffering now "prevents greater evils" later.[5] The greatest danger of all is that we never become aware of our blindness, pride, and self-sufficiency. We naturally believe that we have far more ability to direct our lives wisely than we really have, and that we are far more virtuous, honest, and decent than we really are. These are deadly errors, and Satan would be happy to let you have a charmed and prosperous life for many years so that you don't see the truth until it's too late. God, however, out of love, wants to wake you up to your condition so you can do something about it. In many lives he uses storms.

Years ago, I read an old fairy tale about a wicked witch who lived in a remote cottage in the deep forest.

When travelers came through looking for lodging, she offered them a meal and a bed. It was the most wonderfully comfortable bed any of them had ever felt. But it was a bed full of dark magic, and if you were asleep in it when the sun came up, you would turn to stone. Then you became a figure in the witch's statuary, trapped until the end of time. This witch forced a young girl to serve her, and though she had no power to resist the witch, the girl had become more and more filled with pity for her victims.

One day a young man came looking for bed and board and was taken in. The servant girl could not bear to see him turned to stone. So she threw sticks, stones, and thistles into his bed. It made the bed horribly uncomfortable. Every time he turned he felt a new painful object under him. Though he cast each one out, there was always a new one to dig into his flesh. He slept only fitfully and finally rose, feeling weary and worn, long before dawn. As he walked out the front door, the servant girl met him, and he berated her cruelly. "How could you give a traveler such a terrible bed full of sticks and stones?" he cried and went on his way. "Ah," she said under her breath, "the misery you know now is nothing like the infinitely greater misery a comfortable sleep would have brought upon you! Those were my sticks and stones of love."

God puts sticks and stones of love in our beds to wake us up, to bring us to rely on him, lest the end of history or of life overtake us without the Lord in our hearts, and we be turned to stone. Indeed, the Bible speaks of salvation like this. "I will give you a new heart and put a new spirit in you; I will remove from you your heart of stone and give you a heart of flesh" (Ezekiel 36:26). Self-sufficiency, self-centeredness, self-salvation make us hard toward people we think of as failures and losers, and ironically makes us endlessly self-hating if we don't live up to our standards.[6]

Deep inside the storm and waves that lashed at Jonah, God appointed a great fish to save him. This is a vivid picture of the Romans 8:28 principle. There's love at the heart of our storms. If you turn to God through faith in Christ, he won't let you sink. Why not? Because the only storm that can really destroy—the storm of divine justice and judgment on sin and evil—will never come upon you. Jesus bowed his head into that ultimate storm, willingly, for you. He died, receiving the punishment for sin we deserve, so we can be pardoned when we trust in him. When you see him doing that for you, it certainly does not answer all the questions you have about your suffering. But it proves that, despite it all, he still loves you. Because he was thrown into *that* storm for you, you can be sure that there's love at the heart of *this* storm for you.

> *His love in time past*
> *Forbids me to think*
> *He'll leave me at last*
> *In trouble to sink . . .*

> *By prayer let me wrestle,*
> *and He will perform.*
> *With Christ in the vessel,*
> *I smile at the storm.*[7]

The Pattern of Love (Jonah 1:11–17)

We need not doubt that the New Testament sees Jonah's near death to save the sailors physically as a sign of Jesus's actual death to save us eternally. Commentators have pointed out the fascinating parallels between Jonah's experience in the storm and Jesus's experience in the storm on Lake Galilee in Mark 4:35–41. Both Jesus and Jonah are out on the water in boats. Both Jesus's and Jonah's boats are overtaken by storms. Each storm is described as particularly violent. Both Jesus and Jonah are, surprisingly, asleep in the midst of the mighty storm. In each case, the others in the boat come to the sleeper and cry out to him that they are perishing and that he needs to do something. In Mark 4:38 the disciples seem to express our personal feelings toward God in suffering: "The disciples woke him and said to him, 'Teacher, don't you care if we drown?'" In both Mark 4 and Jonah 1 there is a miraculous intervention by God and the sea is calmed. And finally, after the deliverance, both the sailors and the disciples are described as *more* terrified than they were in the storm (Mark 4:41; Jonah 1:16). These parallels can't be coincidences. By this parallelism, Mark is telling us that Jonah's willingness to die for the sailors points us to an infinitely greater sacrificial love that brings an infinitely greater salvation. Unlike Jonah, Jesus was not thrown into the waters, because Jesus came to save us from a far greater peril than drowning. Jesus was able to calm the storm on Galilee and save his disciples because later, on the cross, he was thrown into the ultimate storm of divine wrath so he could save us from sin and death itself. Jesus himself says, "For as Jonah was three days and three nights in the belly of a huge fish, so the Son of Man will be three days and three nights in the heart of the earth" (Matthew 12:40).

When Jonah told the sailors to throw him overboard, sacrificing himself to save them, he was enacting perhaps the central theme of the Bible. There are at least two aspects of it that we can consider. One aspect is the ethical—that love should be self-giving. We can live life well in this world only through sacrificial love.

New Testament writers took a rather general Greek word for affection—*agape*—and infused it with a new, unique meaning. In the Bible, writes biblical scholar John Stott, "*agape* love means self-sacrifice in the service of others."[8] 1 John 3:16–18 says, "This is how we know what love is: Jesus Christ laid down his life for us. And we ought to lay down our lives for our brothers and sisters." When John says that "this is how we know what love is," he is arguing that, on this side of the cross, love is ever after defined as self-giving. "Just as the essence of hate is murder . . . so the essence of love is self-sacrifice. . . . Murder is taking another person's life; self-sacrifice is laying down one's own."[9]

Many recoil from this definition. The complaint is that it leads some to stay in abusive or exploitative relationships. However, that is to forget the whole definition. Self-sacrifice is always, as Stott says, "in the service of others." Allowing someone to exploit you or sin against you is not loving them at all. It only confirms them in their wrongful behavior and could lead to the ruin of you both. Some people do indeed allow themselves to be browbeaten and used, for many psychologically toxic reasons, all under the guise of being "self-giving." In reality it is selfish, a way to feel superior or needed. To say that self-giving love must lead to abuse and oppression is to misunderstand it entirely.

One of the greatest contrasts between our Western culture and Christianity comes at exactly this point. Our society defines love basically as a transaction for self-fulfillment. It is a market-based definition. You stay in a love relationship as long as both of you are profiting from it. This approach, however, has led to widespread damage.

A recent book on parenting explains why so many modern people are having fewer children or none at all. We are "free to choose or change spouses . . . to choose or change careers. But we can never choose or change [who are] our children. They are the last binding obligation in a culture that asks for almost no other permanent commitments at all."[10] In our individualistic society even marriage has been reshaped into a consumer relationship that exists only so long as each party benefits and profits. As soon as the relationship requires sacrifice on your part—more giving than receiving—society says it can be discarded. Parenting, however, stubbornly resists this modern attitude. It still requires substitutionary sacrifice. You can suffer voluntarily, in love, in a way that gives them life, or they're going to suffer involuntarily for their whole lives.

Another area where the modern view is dysfunctional is in that of reconciliation. No society can hold together if there is not an ability and willingness to forgive. Constant blood feuds and vengeance for past wrongs lay waste to civil society. Yet the ability to set aside grievances and work together requires habits of the heart that our culture no longer forms in us.

In 2006 a lone gunman took hostage ten girls, ages six to thirteen, in an Amish schoolhouse. He shot eight of them, killing five, before committing suicide. The Amish startled the nation when as a community they forgave the killer of their children. They came to the shooter's funeral, expressing support for his traumatized family that he left behind. Also, the individual Amish families that lost children forgave the gunman and his family. While many admired their actions, sociologists studying the event wrote that modern American society can no longer produce people capable of the same response. America, they argued, is now a culture of self-assertion in which all people are encouraged to express themselves and assert their rights. The Amish Christian community, by contrast, had created a culture of self-renunciation, patterned on Jesus's self-sacrifice, renouncing rights in the service of others.[11] Because it has lost the ideal of self-giving and sacrificial love, our society cannot provide its members with the resources for this basic requirement for human life in society.

The second aspect of this theme is the theological. We can be saved eternally only through Christ's sacrificial love.

In literature, plays, and cinema, substitutionary sacrifice is always the most riveting and moving plot point. In the movie *The Last of the Mohicans*, British major Duncan Heyward asks his Indian captors if he might die in the flames so that Cora, whom he loves, and Nathaniel can go free. When, as he is being dragged away, Duncan cries, "My compliments, sir! Take her and get out!" we are electrified by his unflinching willingness to die to save others, one of whom has been his rival. He dies with his arms bound and stretched out, as if he were on a cross.

In Ernest Gordon's memoir of being a prisoner of the Japanese during World War II, he recounts how at the end of a day of forced labor the guards counted the shovels, and one was apparently missing. A furious guard threatened the British POWs that unless the guilty person confessed, he would kill them all. He cocked his gun to start shooting them one by one. At that moment, one prisoner stepped forward calmly and said, "I did it." He stood quietly at attention, and "he did not open his mouth" (Isaiah 53:7) as he was beaten to death. When they all got back to the camp and counted the shovels again, it turned out that they were all there. The man had sacrificed himself to save them all.[12]

In the first Harry Potter novel, the evil Lord Voldemort can't touch Harry without being burned. Later Dumbledore explains it to him. "Your mother died to save you. . . . Love as powerful [as that] . . . leaves its own mark. . . . [T]o have been loved so deeply . . . will give us some protection forever."[13] Why do these stories move us? It's because we know from the mundane corners of life to the most dramatic that all life-changing love is substitutionary sacrifice. We know that anybody who has ever done anything that really made a difference in our lives made a sacrifice, stepped in and gave something or paid something or bore something so we would not have to.

Many today reject the doctrine of substitutionary atonement. They believe it depicts a loving Jesus who extracts forgiveness from a wrathful, reluctant God. Some have called this "divine child abuse." But that insults Jesus. It demotes him into some kind of lesser being, and it is a denial of one of the cardinal doctrines of the Bible and Christianity, namely that there is only one God who exists in three persons, Father, Son, and Holy Spirit. The three persons are not three Gods, but one. So the name "Jesus" means "God saves," and his name "Immanuel" (Matthew 1:21–23) means "God with us." Paul says "that God was reconciling the world to himself in Christ, not counting people's sins against them" (2 Corinthians 5:19). Even while on earth, Christ said that he indwells the Father and the Father indwells him (John 14:11, 17:21–23) and Paul adds that all of the fullness of God dwells in Christ (Colossians 2:9).

What happened on the cross was that God came and substituted himself for us. "The righteous, loving Father humbled himself to become in and through his only Son flesh, sin and a curse for us, in order to redeem us without compromising his own character."[14] In an old Italian church there is a painting of the crucifixion. But behind the body of Christ stretched out on the cross there is the "vast and shadowy Figure" of God so that "the nail that pierces the hand of Jesus goes through to the hand of God. The spear thrust into the side of Jesus goes through into God."[15] The painting shows us a very biblical truth. Paul is able to say that God purchased us "with his own blood" (Acts 20:28). Jesus's blood is God's blood.

And this is the answer to objections about the seeming injustice of substitutionary atonement. John Stott writes:

> *The biblical gospel of atonement is of God satisfying himself by substituting himself for us. The concept of substitution*

may be said, then, to lie at the heart of both sin and salvation. For the essence of sin is man substituting himself for God, while the essence of salvation is God substituting himself for man. Man asserts himself against God and puts himself where only God deserves to be; God sacrifices himself for man and puts himself where only man deserves to be. Man claims prerogatives which belong to God alone; God accepts penalties which belong to man alone.[16]

A God who suffers pain, injustice, and death for us is a God worthy of our worship. In a world of pain and oppression, how could we give our highest allegiance to someone who was immune to all that? This is a God who knows what storms are like because he came into the world and dove straight into the greatest pain and suffering. Because of his self-substitution, we can have life. To the degree you grasp what Jesus did for you, and rest in the salvation he bought for you, to that degree this pattern of substitutionary sacrifice and love will be reproduced in your relationships. And you will become the kind of person the world desperately needs.

CHAPTER 11

OUR RELATIONSHIP TO GOD'S WORLD

Who Is My Neighbor? (Jonah 1:5–6)

One of the main concerns of the book of Jonah is that believers should respect and love their neighbors, including those of a different race and religion. The captain of the ship rebukes Jonah for doing nothing for the common, public good. In the boat during the storm, Jonah contradicts the teaching of Jesus's famous parable of the Good Samaritan (Luke 10:25–37) at every point.

In that story a Samaritan, journeying through a desolate, dangerous place infested with highwaymen, comes upon a Jew who has been attacked, robbed, and left wounded and dying in the road. Jews and Samaritans were enemies, but the Samaritan rescues the wounded man. He then takes him to a place where he can be nursed back to health, all at the Samaritan's expense. With Jonah as a bad example and the Samaritan as the good one, the Bible answers several questions about a believer's social relationships.

Who is my neighbor? By depicting a man helping his enemy and saying, "Go and do likewise," Jesus is telling us in the strongest terms that anyone at all in need, regardless of race, religion, values, and culture, is your neighbor.

How should I regard my neighbor? By making the Samaritan—a member of a people that the Jews considered to be racial outsiders and theological heretics[1]—the hero of the story, Jesus is sending the message that God can and does give gifts of moral goodness, wisdom, and love to all people, all races and classes.

What does it mean to "love my neighbor"? In answering that question, Jesus depicts someone meeting the most practical physical, material, and economic needs. These are needs every human being has, regardless of faith and race. Meeting these needs constitutes the common good, and the Samaritan's actions to seek that common good were extravagant. One commentator sums it up like this:

> *He stops on the Jericho road to assist someone he does not know in spite of the self-evident peril of doing so; he gives of his own goods and money, freely, making no arrangements for reciprocation; in order to obtain care for this stranger, he enters an inn, itself a place of potential danger; and he even enters into an open-ended monetary relationship with the innkeeper, a relationship in which the chance of extortion is high.*[2]

The lengths to which the Samaritan went to help a man of another race and religion were extraordinary, yet Jesus says to us, "Go and do likewise."

Behind Jesus's parable is one of the bedrock truths of the Bible, namely, the teaching that every human being is created in the image and likeness of God (Genesis 1:26–27). While there have been many debates over what specific traits compose the image, it is clear that this makes every human a being of value and worth. Obvious implications are that we must not attack, exploit, or do violence to any person (cf. Genesis 9:6), but the Bible says we must not even curse or treat anyone disrespectfully, because they are in God's image (James 3:9).[3]

John Calvin, who is often thought to be a narrow dogmatician, counters that reputation when he discusses how Christians should regard all their neighbors. He draws remarkable implications from the doctrine of the *imago Dei*. Calvin repeats what he has heard many Christians say to him. A person who is a foreigner deserves no help from them, and many people in their neighborhood are immoral and irreligious, so why should the Christians go out of their way to meet these people's needs? Calvin replies that even those who in themselves deserve nothing but contempt should be treated as if they were the Lord himself, because his image is upon them all. "Say [about the stranger before you] that you owe nothing for any service of his; but God, as it were, has put him in his own place in order that you may recognize toward him the many and great benefits which God has bound you to himself. . . . You will say, 'He has deserved something far different from me.' Yet what has the Lord deserved? . . . *Remember not to consider men's evil intention but to look upon the image of God in them, which cancels and effaces their transgressions, and with its beauty and dignity allures us to love and embrace them."*[4] Calvin's call, that we treat every human being "as the Lord deserves," has some breathtaking practical implications. He goes on to spell them out. "Each [Christian] will so consider with himself . . . a debtor to his neighbors, and that he ought in exercising kindness toward them to set no other limit than the end of his resources."[5]

What does this all mean practically for us? It means that Christians cannot think that their role in life is strictly to build up the church, as crucial as that is. They must also, as neighbors and citizens, work sacrificially for the common life and common good.[6] What is that? In the most basic sense, it refers to things that benefit the entire human community, rather than only the selfish interests of some individuals, groups, or classes. It may refer to:

- a safe environment rather than a community that is plagued by crime or health hazards;

- economic prosperity and humane workplaces rather than a community with few jobs where poverty is rampant;

- a state of peace rather than one marked by violence between individuals, races, groups, or nations;

- a just social order rather than one marked by corruption and by a justice system weighted against the weak or poor;

- publicly available resources such as good educational institutions, medical services, parks, and recreation;

- social harmony and civility in which people from different races, cultures, and moral frameworks relate to one another with respect;

- a community committed to caring for the weak: the elderly, the chronically ill, single parents and orphans, immigrants, and the poor;

- a government that works on behalf of all citizens, not just the rich and powerful.

Christians and Politics

Jonah fled from God rather than seeking the spiritual good of a city he despised. He had allowed himself to become too aligned politically and emotionally with the national security interests of Israel. We must avoid the same error. Nonetheless, after a quick look at the bulleted list above, some will respond that it will be impossible to work for the public or common good without Christians getting involved in politics. That is true, and so a careful balance must be achieved.

First, we must not think it really possible to transcend politics and simply preach the gospel. Those Christians who try to avoid all political discussions and engagement are essentially casting a vote for the social status quo. Since no human society reflects God's justice and righteousness perfectly, supposedly apolitical Christians are supporting many things that displease God. So to not be political is to be political. Churches in the U.S. in the early nineteenth century that did not speak out about slavery because that would have been "getting political" were actually supporting the slavery status quo by staying silent. The Bible also shows us individual believers involved in politics and holding important posts in pagan governments—think of Joseph and Daniel.[7]

Individual Christians can and should be involved politically, as a way of loving our neighbors. To work for better public schools in a poor neighborhood or to end segregation in a country requires political engagement, and Christians have done so and should continue to do so. Nevertheless, while individual Christians must do this, they should not identify the church itself with one set of public policies or one political party as *the* Christian one.[8] There are a number of reasons why.

One reason it is harmful is that it gives listeners to the gospel the strong impression that, to be converted, they not only have to believe in Jesus but also need to become members of the [fill in the blank] party.[9] It confirms what many skeptics want to believe about religion, that it is not a genuine spiritual truth and encounter but only one more political constituency and voting bloc, one more way to get power over others.

Another reason not to align the Christian faith with one party is that most political positions are matters not of biblical prescription but practical wisdom. This does not mean that the church cannot ever speak to social, economic, and political realities, because the Bible does. Racism, as we have seen, is a sin, violating the second commandment to "love thy neighbor." Also, the biblical command to lift up the poor and to defend the rights of the oppressed is not an option for believers; it is a moral imperative. And speaking out against particularly egregious violations of these moral requirements is important.[10]

However, as soon as any group of Christians decides exactly *how* to best pursue these moral ideals in our particular society, they are usually moving beyond biblical prescription into the realm of wisdom and prudence.[11] Is the best way to help the poor to shrink government and let the private capital markets allocate resources, or is it to expand the government and give the state predominance? Efforts to find in the Bible a clear mandate for completely laissez-faire capitalism or for communism fail to convince.[12] The best social policies are somewhere between those poles, but the Bible does not define that point exactly for every time, place, and culture.

I once heard from a friend about a man from Mississippi who was very conservative in every way. He was a conservative Republican; he was also a very traditional Presbyterian. He had long wanted to visit Scotland, the homeland of American Presbyterians. Eventually he arranged to serve for a month as a worker in a little Presbyterian congregation in a village in the Scottish Highlands. The church and its people were as conservative as he expected. They were extremely strict in their observance of the Sabbath. No one so much as turned on a television on Sundays.

However, one day he got into a discussion with several of his admired Scottish Christian friends and discovered, to his shock, that they were all (in his view) socialists. That is, their understanding of tax structure and government economic policy was very left-wing. He couldn't believe it. He had firmly believed that to be conservative theologically meant you were conservative politically on every issue. He spoke long with them and came to learn that their understanding of the role of government was grounded in their Christian convictions. The man came home to the U.S., not any more politically liberal than when he had left but, in his words, "humbled and chastened." He realized that thoughtful Christians, all trying to obey God's call, can reasonably appear at a number of different places on the political spectrum, with loyalties to different political parties.

Another reason why Christians, especially today, cannot allow the church to be fully aligned with any particular party is the problem of "ethical package deals." Many political parties today insist that members commit to *all* the proper positions on all issues. So you cannot align on one issue if you don't embrace the full gamut of all approved positions.[13]

This emphasis on package deals puts pressure on Christians in politics. For example, following both the Bible and the early church, Christians will be committed to racial justice and the poor but also to the understanding that sex is only for marriage.[14] One of those views seems liberal and the other looks oppressively conservative. Christians' positions on social issues, then, do not fit into contemporary political alignments.

As a result, Christians are pushed toward two main options. One is to give up and withdraw, trying to be apolitical. The second possibility is to swallow hard, assimilate, and fully adopt one party's whole package in order to be admitted to the table. Political parties will offer Christian churches, organizations, and leaders heady access to power, support, favors, and protections. All this can be theirs if they support the whole political agenda and look the other way on matters to which Christians ought to object. The spiritual danger here is very great.[15]

Neither of these options is valid. In the Good Samaritan parable, Jesus forbids us to withhold help from our neighbors. On the other hand, if we do experience some exclusion and even persecution (Matthew 5:10), we are assured that some will still see our "good deeds and glorify God" (1 Peter 2:11–12). Our labor in the Lord is never in vain (1 Corinthians 15:58). In fact, if we are *only* offensive or *only* attractive and not both, we can be sure we are failing to live as we ought.

The gospel gives us the ability and the resources to love people who reject both our beliefs and us personally. Think of how God won you over. Not by taking power but by coming and losing power and serving you. How did God save you? He came not with a sword in his hand but with nails in his hands. He came not to bring judgment but to bear judgment. That's why the hymn says:

> *For not with swords loud clashing,*
> *Nor roll of stirring drums;*
> *With deeds of love and mercy*
> *The heavenly kingdom comes.*[16]

The Good Samaritan risked his life and sacrificially loved someone who was not merely a stranger but a member of a racial group that the Samaritan would have seen as dangerous and even responsible for much suffering in his own community. The Jewish man deserved the Samaritan's wrath but instead received sacrificial, practical love, the meeting of his physical and material needs. In this the parable points us to the "Great Samaritan," Jesus Christ. We deserved nothing but his rejection. Indeed, he knew that we, the human race, would put him to death. He did not just risk his life for us—he gave it. He died for us that we might live. Until we see Jesus as our Good Samaritan, we will never be sacrificial in our love for our neighbors.

Embracing the Other (Jonah 1:7–10)

When Jonah introduces himself to the pagan sailors, he puts his racial identity first. This is the first clue that the book gives us of what will be revealed more fully later, namely, that Jonah resents God's mercy given to racial "others." His race and nation have become not merely good things that he loves but idols.

When this happens, it leads us to exclude people who are different from us—to reject, denigrate, avoid, or segregate them or to assimilate them forcibly, demanding they believe and act just like us.[17]

Cultural exclusion seems to happen almost universally. People are shamed and punished in our modern, pluralistic societies if they do not conform to the reigning pieties. For all our talk of tolerance, we demand that others adopt our characteristics and beliefs. They must express no difference from us, or we will name them as beyond the pale of engagement. It is common for us to insist that everyone "respect difference"—allow people to be themselves—but in the very next moment we show complete disrespect for anyone who diverges from our cherished beliefs. We sneer at people more liberal than us as social justice warriors; we disdain those more conservative than us as hateful bigots.

Many argue that tribalism was a survival mechanism and therefore humans are hardwired to get their significance and security from demonizing others.[18]

One author wrote that "one of the most troubling aspects" of human identity is that "the formation of any 'we' must leave out or exclude a 'they,'" so that our identities are inevitably dependent on the people we exclude.[19] Only by denouncing, blaming, and despising people's different identity factors—of race, class, religion, and viewpoint—can we feel good about our own. Exclusion provides us with "the illusion of sinlessness and strength."[20] Exclusion seems to be unavoidable.

Some call for an ideal society of absolute inclusion. They urge us to accept every perspective and equally affirm every kind of person. No one really can tell anyone else what is right or wrong, they say, and so we have to include all viewpoints. Any effort to practice absolute inclusion, however, always leads to new forms of exclusion. You may say, for example, "There are no good people and bad people," but now those who think there *are* good and bad people are the bad people. Supposedly rejecting all "binaries" immediately creates new ones. Also, those who insist on the illusion of total inclusion often demonstrate the inability to name and condemn behavior that is evil or unjust.[21]

So complete inclusion is, in the end, impossible to practice. Everyone ultimately believes in some moral absolutes. Once we realize this, the new question becomes: Which set of beliefs and moral absolutes leads us to embrace most fully those from whom we deeply differ?

Is there anything between the poles of completely affirming all viewpoints and excluding people as "the Other"? Yes, there is. Jesus said: "I tell you, love your enemies and pray for those who persecute you. . . . If you greet only your own people, what are you doing more than others? Do not even pagans do that?" (Matthew 5:44,47). Here Jesus said that his disciples' way of life must contrast sharply with the ordinary way human beings relate to "the Other." Jesus tells us to "greet" all people, and in his time one did this with the word *shalom*. To wish someone *shalom*—the word for full flourishing, health, and happiness—was to want their good. Jesus is acknowledging that some people are indeed opponents, even persecutors. He does not say that everyone is equally right and good, but he does insist that their needs as human beings are equally important, regardless of their beliefs. He charges his disciples to open their hearts to those who are different, and to make space for them in their attention, emotions, and lives.

As we have seen, many will claim that this is simply impossible, that our identities are irreducibly based on feeling superior to groups and persons whom we see as inferior. But this should not be true in the case of those who claim a Christian identity.

Ordinarily, human identity and self-worth come from our achievements. We are proud of being a successful professional, or we are proud of being part of a racial group that has so many great accomplishments. We build up the self-esteem of individuals and groups by showering them with praise for their attainments. But such an identity is inherently fragile and unstable. It needs constant recognition and shoring up. Most religious identities are the same. We may say, "I have worked hard at prayer, at studying religious doctrine, at living a good life, and so I think I can say that I know God."

Christian identity, however, is received, not achieved. In C. S. Lewis's *The Chronicles of Narnia*, one of the characters is asked if he knows Aslan, a lion who is the Christ figure of the books. He answers, "Well—he knows me."[22] This echoes Paul's statement to the Galatian Christians, "But now that you know God—or rather are known by God" (Galatians 4:9). Keep in mind that to know someone in the Bible does not mean simply to know about but to be in a personal relationship. What makes a person a Christian is not our love for God, which is always imperfect, but God's love for us. To ground your identity in your own efforts and accomplishments—even in the amount of love you have for Jesus—is to have an unstable, fragile identity. We are usually in doubt as to whether we have been good enough, and even if we have had a good week, we fear that next week may be worse.

However, when we put our faith in Christ, we are fully received and accepted by God on the basis of Christ's work, not ours (2 Corinthians 5:21). We are adopted into God's family (John 1:12–13) and we are loved by God with the unconditional love of a parent, not the conditional regard of an employer or a mere sovereign. This puts our self-worth on an entirely new footing. With Paul we can say that in ourselves we are "unworthy" but "by the grace of God I am what I am" (1 Corinthians 15:10). Because our security and assurance of being loved do not rest in our performance, we have the psychological freedom to do what Jonah could not do—to look into our hearts, recognize our flaws, and admit them (Romans 7:21–25). Yet despite such heightened awareness of our sinfulness, a Christian is not without great confidence. Paul says that Christians "boast"—we get courage—from looking not at our own strength or attainments but at how we are regarded in Christ (1 Corinthians 1:31; Galatians 6:14; Philippians 3:3).

This new understanding of who we are in Christ transforms how we relate to people who are different from us.

Christians still have the same jobs, the same families, the same racial and ethnic backgrounds, yet God's love in Christ now becomes the most fundamental source of our self-worth. This displaces, but does not efface or remove, our other identity factors. So Paul says, on the one hand, that in Christ "there is neither Jew nor Gentile" (Galatians 3:28), and yet as a Jew he still embraced his unique cultural customs and patterns (Acts 21:24–26). That means that when you become a Christian you don't stop being Chinese or European, but now your race and nation don't define you as fully as they did. You do not rely on them for worth and honor in the same way. You are a Christian first and Chinese or European second. Being a Christian gives you some distance and objectivity so you can see both the good and the bad parts of your culture more clearly than many who are still relying on it for their fundamental self-worth.

> *Christians can never be first of all Asians or Americans, Russians or Tutsis, and then Christians. . . . When they respond to the call of the gospel they put one foot outside their culture while the other remains firmly planted in it. [Christianity] is not flight from one's original culture, but a new*

way of living within it because of the new vision of peace and joy in Christ.[23]

I came to experience all this directly some years ago when I visited a church meeting in a poor black township in South Africa. There I visited with the leaders and members of a small church. One of the pillars of that church was a single mother who had faced great deprivation, oppression, and suffering over the years. Yet her faith had not simply helped her to cope with all these things; she had triumphed over them. The hardships of her life had not made her bitter, or cynical and hard, or weak and dependent. She was a radiant Christian, filled with confidence in God and sacrificial love for others.

Though I was a minister in a large church in a big city, I was able to recognize in her someone who was my superior in prayer and faith in Jesus. If I had not been a Christian, as a white American male I would have had little more than pity for her. She had not started any new organizations or campaigns. She was not a great political leader. She had none of the traits that I would have valued most. However, I am now a Christian first and a white American second, and because of our common bond in Christ, I recognized a sister who was equal with me as a sinner saved by grace and who excelled me in many crucial ways. This meant I was able to listen to her in a way I would not have done otherwise. That experience then had spill-over effect—I began to regard other marginalized people with a new understanding I could not have discovered in any other way.

The early Christians startled the Roman world with this unique facet of their identity. Until that time, one's religion and faith were nothing but an extension of one's national identity. Your race determined who your gods were—race came first and religion was just a way of expressing it. Christians said that their God was the God of the whole world, and that people of all races could be Christians, and that therefore faith was more important than race.[24] The early Christian churches were multiethnic in an unprecedented way. They brought together people who would never have gotten along before they believed in Christ.

This is not a lesson that Jonah ever learned within the time frame of this story. At the very last moment God is urging him to see it. However, we have far less excuse than Jonah if we fall into *othering* people of different races and cultures.

In J. R. R. Tolkien's *The Lord of the Rings*, one of the main characters, Gimli the Dwarf, shares with his whole race a distrust and dislike of the Elves. In Tolkien's narrative, Elves and Dwarves have had centuries of strife in their past. Then Gimli comes to the land of Lórien and stands before the Elf queen Galadriel. Though he is wretched and sad, she speaks words of encouragement to him in his own secret language, a tongue the Dwarves teach to no one. Gimli is amazed at her knowledge of him and the generous gesture.

> *And the Dwarf, hearing the names given in his own ancient tongue, looked up and met her eyes; and it seemed to him that he looked suddenly into the heart of an enemy and saw there love and understanding. Wonder came into his face, and then he smiled in answer.*

He rose clumsily and bowed in dwarf-fashion, saying, "Yet more fair is the land of Lórien, and the Lady Galadriel is above all the jewels that lie beneath the earth!"[25]

After this, in the rest of the book, Gimli's attitude toward the whole Elvish race begins to change, and he is freed to become closest friends with another Elf, Legolas. When he is embraced in love by an Other whom he thought was an enemy, it transforms him and enables him to welcome others who are deeply different from himself.

When Jesus calls us in the Sermon on the Mount to love our enemies and greet those who are different, he is not asking us to do anything that he did not do himself. He was Other from us—he was "in very nature God" (Philippians 2:6). He was the deity whose holy presence daunted Moses and Isaiah (Exodus 3:1–14; Isaiah 6:1–9) and whose glory was fatal if seen (Exodus 33:20). Yet Jesus, the wholly Other, became the same as us.

Who, being in very nature God, did not consider equality with God something to be used to his own advantage; rather, he made himself nothing by taking the very nature of a servant, being made in human likeness. And being found in appearance as a man, he humbled himself by becoming obedient to death—even death on a cross (Philippians 2:6–8)!

Here we have the model for loving and welcoming those who are deeply different, rather than excluding them as Other. Jesus certainly had the right to exclude us, but he did not. He loved, welcomed, and reconciled us to himself—all the while not merely affirming us in some general sense but calling us to radical repentance. He neither included us as if we had a right to be welcomed nor excluded and rejected us as our sins deserved. His voluntary sacrificial death to pay the penalty for our sins both convicts us of sin and the need to change and assures us of his love and pardon despite our flaws, at once.[26]

Here, then, is the model for how we should treat those who are different. Here is also the power to do it. When Paul was on the road to Damascus, on his way to imprison and execute more Christians, Jesus appeared to him and said that by persecuting Christians Paul was persecuting *him* (Acts 9:5). Paul was Christ's enemy. Yet Christ forgave him and healed his physical and spiritual blindness. Paul encountered one who should have treated him as an enemy but found love. When the one you thought to be "the Other" has not treated *you* as Other but given himself in love for you, how can you ever treat anyone else as an enemy? The fear and insecurity that generate the need to protect and justify one's self-worth will be gone.

In 2004 the Dutch filmmaker Theo van Gogh was killed by a Muslim radical. In the aftermath of his death, both churches and mosques in the Netherlands experienced retaliatory attacks, including the bombing of an Islamic school. The outpouring of violent rage shook a Dutch nation that had prided itself on being a peaceful and open society.[27] At this incendiary moment, a Dutch Protestant minister, Reverend Kees Sybrandi, did something radical. Sybrandi was a very conservative, traditional Dutchman who lived in a community where poor Middle Eastern immigrants had brought much poverty and crime.[28] Yet that week

Sybrandi "walked to his neighborhood mosque. He knocked firmly on the door, and to the shock of the Muslims huddled inside, he announced that he would stand guard outside the mosque every night until the . . . attacks ceased. In the days and weeks that followed, the minister called on other churches in the area and they joined him, circling and guarding the mosques throughout the region for more than three months."[29]

Why would Sybrandi have done such a thing? One interviewer tried to find out. Was it some experience that had made the change? No. The minister "recounted no stories of past friendships or dialogues with Muslims." Perhaps the secular, liberal values had softened him? No. "Multicultural appeals for a celebration of difference had little pull on his heart." So what had overcome his inherent traditionalism and temperamental conservatism? "[He] simply replied 'Jesus. Jesus commanded me to love my neighbor—[and even] my enemy too."[30]

And on what basis did Jesus command such a

thing? Christ tells us we must be gracious to others because we have received grace ourselves. In his parable of the Unmerciful Servant, he tells us that Christians who know they live wholly by God's undeserved mercy *must* be generous, forgiving, and welcoming to all others, even those whom they see as opponents (Matthew 18:21–35).

Doing Justice, Preaching Wrath (Jonah 3:1–10)

The mission of Jonah to Nineveh bristles with practical lessons for us.

There is the lesson about *mission.*

Jonah's call to leave his homeland to preach God's Word was unprecedented in the Old Testament, but this is the mandate given to all believers by Jesus (Matthew 28:18–20). So while we are not all called to be preachers or prophets or missionaries, every believer is called to *go.* It means to be willing to leave safety and security in order to share the good news of

Jesus with others. This may or may not entail leaving physical and social locations, but it always means risk and vulnerability.

Mission is not only for a spiritual elite, or for the well rested, or for people with the gift of gab, or for outgoing personalities, or for those with theological training. It is for every person who belongs to him. It is because God is by nature a sending God. He never calls us in to bless us without also sending us out to be a blessing to others.

The first and great example of this is the father of all the faithful, Abraham. God came and said to him, "Go from your country, your people and your father's household to the land I will show you. I will make you into a great nation and I will bless you . . . and you will be a blessing . . . [for] all peoples on earth will be blessed through you" (Genesis 12:1–3). God called Abraham to leave his familiar culture ("your people") and his personal and emotional security ("your father's household"). That is, he is called to abandon everything he has relied on for meaning and security. Here's an outline of his life:

"Go." *Where?* "I'll tell you later. Just go."

(GENESIS 12)

"You will have a son." *How?*
"I'll tell you later. Just trust."

(GENESIS 15)

"Offer up your son on the mount." *Why?* "I'll
tell you later. Just climb."

(GENESIS 22)

We may respond that Abraham was a unique fore-father and Jonah was a Hebrew prophet and that their calls to mission, to go into uncertainty and insecurity, are not for all of us. However, Hebrews 11:8–10 uses Abraham's answer to God's call away from security as a model for all believers. Verse 8 says that when God called Abraham to go out, "By faith [he] . . . obeyed and went, even though he did not know where he was going." Why did he do it? Verse 10 answers: "For he was looking forward to the city with foundations, whose architect and builder is God." It is only God's kingdom that has "foundations" that will last. It is only God's approval, God's protection, and God's eternal inheritance that are permanent. So if we think we might look foolish to someone if we talk about our faith, or if we think that the needs of a particular ministry or mission may require sacrificial financial giving—and we do what is necessary—we are answering the same call away from security that God gives to all who believe. The call to both Abraham and Jonah, then, is a model for us.

Also, there is a lesson about *cities*.

Jonah undertook what we could call an urban mission. He went to a city that was one of the largest in the world at that time. When God is arguing about why he should be deeply concerned for Nineveh, he cites its population figure as a reason for the city's significance to him and uses the term *adam*—the word for humankind: "120,000 of humanity." It is as if God was saying, "I care about human beings, and so how much more should I be concerned to reach a place where so much humanity is amassed?"

This simple logic is powerful. Many people simply do not like cities, but if we care about people, and if we believe that the deepest human need is to be reconciled to God, then all Christians must be concerned for and supportive of urban Christian ministry in one way or another. If anything, God's appeal to sheer size as an indicator of spiritual need comes home to us today with greater force. At the beginning of the nineteenth century only 5 percent of the world's population lived in cities, a percentage that grew to 14 percent by 1900. The number is over 50 percent today and is on the way to perhaps 80 percent by 2050.[31] In 1950 Shenzhen, China, had a population of 3,148 and Kinshasa (then called Léopoldville), Congo, had 200,000. By 2025 the United Nations predicts the two cities will have grown to 12 million and 16 million, respectively. During that same time Latin America's population has gone from being less than 40 percent urban to over 80 percent.[32] In the West, cities are growing much more slowly, but most are growing in their centers, attracting young adults and new immigrants, and in general they are more secular and resistant to Christian witness than other places.

This is "the most massive migration of people in

the whole of history" and, as two international observers point out, "there is a massive imbalance in the proportion of Christian resources devoted to Christian presence, witness, and mission in the huge and growing cities of the [global] South."[33] Surely God calls Christians and churches to go and live everywhere that there are people, but the people of the world are moving into the city much faster than the church is going.[34] "This context may give a special resonance to God's final . . . question to Jonah, *Should I not be concerned about Nineveh, that great city?*"[35]

One of the reasons that believers today dislike cities is because they are often places of great opposition to Christianity. Cities are seldom hotbeds of orthodox faith, and many young Christians move to cities and lose their faith. Some today believe that Christians should remove themselves from these centers of unbelief.

Jonah was called to have compassion on a city that was a threat to his people (Jonah 4:11). Years later, God made the same call to believers to seek the common good of a pagan city that already *had* done violence to their nation (Jeremiah 29:4–7). The Babylonian empire had invaded and sacked Jerusalem, carrying off many of its people into exile. The strategy of the Babylonians was to assimilate the Jews culturally so they would lose their faith, culture, and view of the world.[36] To counter this strategy, there were prophets, such as Hannaniah (Jeremiah 28:1–17), who called the Jews to remain outside the city. This was a sort of tribalism in which the city was despised and hated and dealt with only to the degree necessary to build up your own economy. Ironically, both assimilation and tribalism are radically selfish. There is no love for the city—in both cases the city is being used to build up wealth, status, and power.

God rejects both assimilation and tribalism for his people. He forbids both blending in and withdrawal. Instead he says:

> *This is what the Lord Almighty, the God of Israel, says to all those I carried into exile from Jerusalem to Babylon: "Build houses and settle down; plant gardens and eat what they produce. Marry and have sons and daughters; find wives for your sons and give your daughters in marriage, so*

that they too may have sons and daughters. Increase in number there; do not decrease. Also, seek the peace and prosperity of the city to which I have carried you into exile. Pray to the Lord for it, because if it prospers, you too will prosper" (Jeremiah 29:4–7).

This must have been an enormous shock. Some of the leaders of Babylon had hands stained with the blood of the Jews' kindred. Idols and false gods filled the city. Yet God had the audacity to tell them to become deeply involved with the city, seeking its peace and prosperity, all the while not compromising on their beliefs and faithfulness to him at all. Either withdrawal or assimilation is easier. Seeking the common good, yet without any compromise of faith and practice, is much more difficult. Yet that is God's call to his people.

This model—of exiles seeking the common good of their city—is also the model given to the New Testament Church. Both Peter and James call Christians "exiles" (James 1:1; 1 Peter 1:1). Peter uses *parapidêmos*, a word that means "resident aliens." *Parapidêmoi* were citizens of one country yet full-time residents of another. Christians are citizens of "the Jerusalem that is above" (Galatians 4:22–26; cf. Philippians 3:20 "our citizenship is in heaven"), and yet we are to also pray for and seek the well-being of our earthly cities.

Finally, there is a lesson about *justice.*

We have seen that Jonah's preaching to Nineveh resulted not so much in conversions (although we cannot be sure there were none) as in social reform. The brutal society promised to turn away from its violence (Jonah 3:8). The prophets' messages to the Gentile nations ordinarily consisted of a denunciation of their exploitive social practices and a call to do justice. What does the Bible mean when it calls people to "seek justice" and "defend the oppressed" (Isaiah 1:17)?

It means seeking equal treatment for all. Leviticus 24:22 tells believers that they must have "the same law for the foreigner and the native-born." You are promoting injustice if you privilege one race or nationality over another, or citizens over immigrants. A host of other biblical texts denounce any judicial system weighted in favor of the wealthy while disenfranchising the poor (cf. Isaiah 1:23–24).

It means having a special concern for economically and socially vulnerable groups. Proverbs 31:8–9 says: "Speak up for those who cannot speak for themselves, for the rights of all who are destitute. . . . Defend the rights of the poor and needy" (cf. Zechariah 7:9–10). It does not say, "Speak up for the rich and powerful," not because they do not merit equal treatment—they do—but because the Bible here is concerned with distributing power to those without it.

Finally, doing justice means broad-based, radical generosity. When Isaiah 58:6 calls us to "loose the chains of injustice and . . . set the oppressed free," the next verse defines that as "to share your food with the hungry, and to provide the [homeless] with shelter." When Job is recounting the admirable life he has lived, he says that he did not put his trust in gold, saying "'you are my security'" (Job 31:24), but rather shared his bread, clothing, and other possessions with the poor (verses 16–19). It is unjust to fail to share with the poor. This lack of just generosity can take other forms. Exploiting your employees, paying them an ungenerous wage, is considered injustice (Isaiah 58:6–7). Whatever you have is only by God's gift and appointment (1 Chronicles 29:12–14). So to not share what you have with those who have less—to fail to meet their basic human needs like food, safe housing, health, and education—is being not simply unmerciful but unjust.

The book of Jonah shows not only that justice was important to God but also the preaching of repentance and God's wrath. How, practically speaking, can we combine evangelism and doing justice?

One proposed model is to see these two things as "two wings on an airplane." While that analogy conveys the necessity of both, it does not describe how integral they are, how one leads to the other. Another model sees helping the needy as a mere means to an end. We give people things so they will turn to Christ. That does not fit with Jesus's teachings that we should give without expecting in return (Luke 6:32–35) and that we should serve the needs of our neighbor even if he or she does not share our faith (Luke 10:25–37). A third mistake is to insist that doing justice is all we need to do to declare God's good news, as if helping the marginalized *were* evangelism. Nor should we treat justice as optional work that we may get to if we have the time or money. All of these very common formulations lack biblical nuance.

We must realize that since all our social problems stem from our alienation from God (Genesis 3:1–17), the most radical and loving thing you can do for a person is to see him or her reconciled to God. Yet while preaching repentance is fundamental, doing justice must be inseparably attached to it. If you have a new relationship with God, it *must* affect all your other relationships. The Old Testament prophets regularly declared that while you may be religious and fast and pray, if you don't do justice, your religion is a sham (Isaiah 58:1–7). Isaiah said that if we don't care for the poor, then we may seem to honor God with our lips but our hearts are far from him (Isaiah 29:13).

The New Testament is no different. Like the prophets, Jesus condemns people who make lengthy prayers but exploit the poor (Mark 12:38,40). And both 1 John 3:17–18 and James 2:14–17 likewise state that if you say you have faith in Jesus but see someone "without clothes and daily food" and do nothing for "physical needs," such faith is "dead." All this is to say that compassion for the poor is an inevitable sign of a living relationship with God and an experience of God's grace. While it does not initiate God's favor and acceptance, it is a sure symptom of having experienced his love. Those who truly know they have eternal life only because of the free, charitable grace of God will be charitable.

So preaching repentance is fundamental, but doing justice must be inseparably connected to it. This combination of doing justice and preaching judgment—and therefore offering grace—goes together not only theologically and philosophically but also practically.

When the world sees the church doing evangelism, making converts, it only sees us increasing our tribe, adding to our numbers and increasing our power. When it sees us sacrificially serving the needs of our neighbors *whether they believe as we do or not*, then it may begin to see that believers are motivated more by love than by the desire to accrue power. In Christian theology our belief in the God of judgment and grace is the basis for doing justice in our society. In the eyes of those outside the church, it is Christians' doing justice that makes belief in the gospel plausible. Doing justice for our neighbors, whether they believe in Christ or not is, paradoxically, one of the best recommendations for the faith. Like Jesus, we must be mighty in both word and deed (Luke 24:19).

They also go together philosophically. Our Western culture is secular, so it is widely believed that moral values are socially constructed rather than God given. As it is commonly asserted, "No one has the right to tell anyone else what is right or wrong for him or her." It is a cultural given that every person determines his or her own moral values. Nevertheless, it is just as strongly believed that all people are obligated to support equal rights, justice for all, and care for the poor. This is one of the great contradictions of our society today. It insists that all morality is relative and then it demands moral behavior. What if someone has the temerity to ask, "*Why* should I sacrifice my time and money for people far off who are starving? Why do I have any obligation to embrace people of other races and beliefs? Why should I be unselfish?" The culture can manage only two answers, both inadequate. The first answer is that to do so serves your own selfish interests. Many thinkers have pointed out the foolishness of basing self-sacrificial behavior on pragmatic self-interest. The other answer is that these values are simply self-evident, but for many people in the world they are not.

These modern beliefs—that we must all be committed to equal rights and justice but that there are no God-given moral absolutes—undermine each other. Modern secular education teaches every child that they must be true to themselves, that they must identify their deepest desires and dreams and pursue them, not letting family, community, tradition, or religion stand in their way. Then it calls for justice, reconciliation, and benevolence, all of which are basic forms of self-denial, even as it encourages self-assertion. It teaches relativism and calls people to be ethical. It encourages self-seeking and calls people to be sacrificial. As C. S. Lewis says:

> *We continue to clamor for those very qualities we are rendering impossible. . . . In a sort of ghastly simplicity we remove the organ and demand the function. . . . We laugh at honor and are shocked to find traitors in our midst. We castrate and bid the geldings be fruitful.*[37]

Christians can make a major contribution here. The philosopher Charles Taylor, in his book *Sources of the Self: The Making of the Modern Identity*, points out that modern society is "on the deepest level incoherent" with regard to morality.[38] Our culture demands impartial benevolence toward all people, social justice for every oppressed class, and the reduction of hunger, disease, and suffering everywhere in the world, "while [at the same time] in principle denying that any such moral value is other than an arbitrary, subjective preference."[39] One reviewer of *Sources of the Self*, himself an atheist, admits that Taylor's thesis makes him very uncomfortable. He writes:

Perseverance in virtue will . . . require self-sacrifice. And self-sacrifice seems to require some transcendental justification or motivation, of which the most common, and perhaps the most logical, is belief in the existence of God. Or so Taylor argues, circumspectly. Since modern freedom entails the rejection of transcendence, modern virtue is wholly contingent. Can we be good for long without God? Taylor's doubts are daunting.[40]

Christians, of course, share all those moral commitments—to human rights, equal human dignity, universal benevolence, and the interests of the poor. Indeed, it is widely and well argued that those values were imported by secular, modern society from the Bible. Christians have the resources for "perseverance in virtue" and self-sacrifice. They come not just from belief in God and the afterlife in general but from every feature of the Christian gospel—the incarnation of Christ, his atoning death on the cross, and the hope of the resurrection. The more Christians draw on these resources and love their neighbors, the stronger society can be.

CHAPTER 12

ᏬᎨᎧᎨᏫ

OUR RELATIONSHIP TO GOD'S GRACE

Running from Grace (Jonah 2:1–10)

One of the messages of this book is that anyone, even a successful prophet (or preacher), can be in the dark about grace. Jonah's fears, prejudices, and emotional breakdown all stem from his blindness to the reality of grace. In chapter 1 he runs away because he finds God's grace and mercy an inexplicable mystery. In chapter 2, in the belly of the fish, we find him wrestling with that same mystery. It is only when he has a breakthrough in his understanding about grace that he is released. Only then can he become a fearless preacher. The main purpose of God is to get Jonah to understand grace. The main purpose of the book of Jonah is to get *us* to understand grace.

If Jonah failed to understand the mystery of God's grace, it is most certainly possible for us. Ignorance of the depth of God's grace causes our most severe problems. Until we understand it, we are, like Jonah, just a shadow of what we could be and should be. The doctrine of the grace of God is that which sets Christianity apart from all other faiths. It is the central message, the "gospel." "The gospel is bearing fruit and growing throughout the whole world—just as it has been doing among you since the day you heard it and truly understood God's grace" (Colossians 1:6).

It is an understanding of God's grace that makes a person a Christian and not merely a moral person or a religious person or a nice person. This is a truth that, when it is grasped, is electrifying. When Martin Luther finally understood it, he went from being an anxious, guilt-ridden seminary professor to a lion ready to take on the whole world by himself. He wrote:

Faith is a living, bold trust in God's grace, so certain of God's favor that it would risk death a thousand times trusting in it. Such confidence and knowledge of God's grace makes you happy, joyful and bold in your relationship to God and all creatures. The Holy Spirit makes this happen through faith. Because of it, you freely, willingly and joyfully do good to everyone, serve everyone, suffer all kinds of things, love and praise the God who has shown you such grace.[1]

It is an understanding of God's grace that makes it possible to take a hard stand. Dietrich Bonhoeffer, in trying to understand how so much of the German church was willing to accept Hitler, identified the problem as "cheap grace."[2] They believed that God loved them despite their sins, but that led to an attitude that ultimately it didn't matter how they lived. Standing up against Hitler at that time would have been dangerous. Many therefore reasoned, "Well, maybe it's cowardly and maybe it's wrong. But God will overlook it. He accepts us despite our sin." As Heinrich Heine, the nineteenth-century writer, was reputed to have said when he was dying, "God will forgive me. That's his job."[3] If you believe that—that God just forgives us and overlooks sin with a shrug—then you will take sin lightly because apparently God does too. However, if you realize that our salvation cost Jesus his glory in heaven and his life on earth, that it entailed unimaginable suffering for him, then you begin to understand that grace is not cheap but costly (Philippians 2:1–11).

Unless we see what it cost him to save us, we won't be glad to obey and serve him, regardless of the cost to us. Packer writes:

> *Those who suppose that the doctrine of God's grace tends to encourage moral laxity . . . are simply showing that, in the most literal sense, they do not know what they are talking about. For love awakens love in return; and love, once awakened, desires to give pleasure.*[4]

And what gives God delight? It is when we stop boasting about and getting our identity from human wisdom, might, and wealth and begin to live in generosity, justice, and righteousness. "For in these I delight, declares the Lord" (Jeremiah 9:23–24).

It is an understanding of God's grace that removes our burdens. Religious people often invite nonbelievers to convert by calling them to adopt new sets of behaviors and new ritual practices, all the while redoubling their efforts to live a virtuous life. That, however, is to load more burdens on people. The Pharisees did this, laying "heavy, cumbersome loads" on people (Matthew 23:4), and so they sank. All other religions put on people the burden of securing their own salvation, while God provides unearned salvation through his son (cf. Isaiah 46:1–4). While the gospel must lead to a changed life, it is not those changes that save you.

A group of young men around John and Charles Wesley in the 1730s struggled to know and serve God. They began reading aloud Martin Luther's commentary on the Galatians. One night, one of the men, William Holland, had an experience of grace that he wrote about later.

Mr. Charles Wesley read the Preface aloud. At the words, "What, have we then nothing to do? No! Nothing but only accept of Him, Who of God is made unto us wisdom and righteousness and sanctification and redemption," there came such a power over me as I cannot well describe; my great burden fell off in an instant; my heart was so filled with peace and love that I burst into tears. I almost thought I saw our Savior! My companions, perceiving me so affected, fell on their knees and prayed. When I afterwards went into the street, I could scarcely feel the ground I trod upon.[5]

Charles Wesley himself had a similar experience, also through the writings of Luther. And he wrote about it like this:

Long my imprisoned spirit lay
fast bound in sin and nature's night.
Thine eye diffused a quickening ray.
I woke. My dungeon flamed with light.
My chains fell off, my heart was free
I rose, went forth, and followed Thee.[6]

Grace becomes, as it were, the background music of your life. If that is the song your heart sings much of the time, it changes you (Ephesians 5:19–20).

How can God be so merciful, patient, and gracious? A clue to the answer is embedded in Jonah's prayer, where he cries:

Out of the belly of Sheol I cry, and you hear my voice. For you cast me into the deep. . . . All your waves and your billows pass over me. . . . I am driven away from your sight (Jonah 2:2–4).

"Sheol" meant the realm of divine punishment and death.[7] Jack Sasson says that to speak of already being in such a place expresses extreme anguish and pain. The metaphor is "unique to Jonah and conveys despair of the darkest hue."[8] Jonah knows his suffering is a penalty, that his sin banished him from God's sight.

When Jesus calls himself "greater than Jonah," he refers to the three days and three nights of Jonah in the deep (Matthew 12:40–41). For on the cross Jesus recapitulates the suffering of Jonah, but to an infinitely greater degree when he cries out, "My God, my God, why have you forsaken me?" (Matthew 27:46). Jonah went into the depths of the sea in order to save the sailors, but Jesus went into the depths of death and separation from God—hell itself—in order to save Jonah. Jonah is crushed under the weight of the "waves and breakers" (verse Jonah 2:3) of God's "waters" (verse 5), but Jesus was buried under the waves and billows of God's wrath. Jonah said he was in Sheol and driven from God's sight. The Apostles' Creed says that, for our sake, Jesus "descended into hell." A classic explanation of that line:

> The point is that the Creed sets forth what Christ suffered in the sight of men, and then appositely speaks of that invisible and incomprehensible judgment which he underwent in the sight of God in order that we might know not only that Christ's body was given as the price of our redemption, but that he paid a greater and more excellent price in suffering in his soul the terrible torments of a condemned and forsaken man.[9]

Whatever your problem, God solves it with his grace. God's grace abolishes guilt forever. You may be filled with regret for the past or you may be living with a sense of great failure. It doesn't matter what you have done. If you were a hundred times worse than you are, your sins would be no match for his mercy. There is a hymn that goes: "Well might the Accuser roar / Of sins that I have done / I see them all and thousands more." Yet if you are in Christ, "Jehovah knoweth none."[10]

Grace abolishes fear of failure, which may have been part of Jonah's problem. So many of our deepest longings to succeed are really just ways to be for ourselves what Christ should be for us. Really we are saying, "If I achieve this, then I am acceptable!" But when we stop trying to steal self-acceptance from other sources, we lose our fear. We become fearless without becoming defiant.

Salvation belongs to the Lord. It is all from him. It is not partly from you and partly from him. It is from him. If you feel, "I wish I were more worthy," you still don't understand it. He *is* your worthiness. If you say, "I want him in my life but I don't see him working," you still don't understand how fundamental his grace is. If you want it at all, that is God working in your life. You are not capable of wanting him on your own. Salvation is of the Lord.

Heart Storms (Jonah 4:1–3)

We have seen that Jonah's angry relapse has to do with an inordinate concern for his nation's political fortunes. One could say he fell into a kind of extreme partisanship, where he would rather have people destroyed and spiritually lost as long as it benefited his country. We could also say, as many have, that Jonah was at best a jingoist and at worst a racist. The danger in doing so is that, while such denunciation may make us feel virtuous, we must also do justice to the rightful love of country and attachment to one's people and culture that is good.

C. S. Lewis's set of essays *The Four Loves* is famous

for what it says on the subjects of friendship and sex. Less well known is his treatment of patriotism. Lewis had served his country in World War I. He was wounded and lost comrades. He felt pride and love for his nation and land. Yet he begins his discussion of "love of country" by saying, "We all know now that this love becomes a demon when it becomes a god."[11] Lewis was referring to Nazism, a form of intense patriotism that had become demonic.

Lewis says that, in response to the horrors visited on the world by overblown nationalism, "some begin to expect that [love of country] is never anything but a demon." Certainly today in Western culture that sentiment has grown. On many college and university campuses virtually any expression of national pride is seen as a fascist and/or racist. But Lewis rejects anti-patriotism as just another form of extremism. Those who see love of nation as always toxic "have to reject half the high poetry and half the heroic action our race has achieved." He adds, strikingly, "We cannot even keep Christ's lament over Jerusalem [where] He too exhibits love for his country."[12]

Instead, Lewis leads us wisely to break down patriotism or love of country into several aspects or kinds, some of which are less likely than others to lead to cruelty and oppression.

The first kind is "love of home"—love of the places we grew up, of the types of people who live there, of the landscape, the sights and sounds, the food and smells and way of life. Lewis thinks that this kind of love of country is the least likely to produce animosity toward those who are different. Appreciation of the things that make your place unique helps you to imagine others loving their distinct places in the same way.

The second kind of love of country is "a particular attitude to our country's past . . . the great deeds of our ancestors." He says that this already presents a danger. It is tempting to airbrush our history and hide how "the actual history of every country is full of shabby and even shameful doings." When that happens we lose a sense that our nation and culture is, like all others, a mix of good and evil people and elements. Here is where a sense of national superiority may begin to breed, along with a potential to believe that *our race* inherits this superiority automatically.[13]

Lewis believes that when a nation intentionally suppresses and erases its own historical misdeeds, this can lead, thirdly, to conscious and deliberate feelings of racial superiority. He remembers a time when he heard a man explicitly voice English superiority to other countries and cultures. Lewis responded, perhaps with a bit of humor, that every country likes to think its people the bravest and fairest in the world, to which the man replied without irony, "Yes, but in England it's true."[14] Here, Lewis says, we are on the doorstep of racism and oppression. "If our country's cause is the cause of God, wars must be wars of annihilation. [This is what happens when] a false transcendence is given to things which are very much of this world."[15]

The final stage of this pathway—from healthy love of one's home and country to making one's race and nation into a god—comes when a race or country uses the premise of its superiority as a basis for cruelty, oppression, exclusion, and even extermination. "Dogs! Know your betters!"[16]

The pathway from a healthy love to a toxic patriotism that Lewis lays out has a number of stages, and it appears Jonah is moving through them. We know from history that Assyria eventually destroyed the ten northern tribes of Israel. So Jonah was not unrealistic in his fears. Yet God was calling him to put his Word and the spiritual good of people ahead of Israel's interests.

Jonah's love for his people and his patriotism— which were good things—had turned sour. His love of his people had become bigotry, and now, without the hope that Israel would win this international power struggle, his life had lost all meaning. As long as serving God fit into his goals for Israel, he was fine with God. As soon as he had to choose between the true God and the god he actually worshipped, he turned on the true God in anger. Jonah's particular national identity was more foundational to his self-worth than his role as a servant of the God of all nations. The real God had been just a means to an end. He was using God to serve his real god.[17]

Race and nation are just two of an infinite number of good things that can become idols. The philosopher Paul Tillich argued that everyone must live for something in order that life have meaning, and whatever that thing is becomes "the ultimate concern." Tillich doubted, therefore, that true, thorough atheism was really possible. He argued that if you don't call the meaning of your life a god, it still functions like one and therefore everyone's life is based on faith.[18] In the same vein, the postmodern novelist David Foster Wallace said that in daily life "there is no such thing as . . . not worshipping." He went on to say that "where[ever] you tap real meaning in life"—whether it is having enough money, being beautiful (or having a beautiful partner), or being thought smart or promoting some political cause—"everybody worships. The only choice we get is what to worship." Wallace knew that modern, secular people would protest very strongly that they are *not* worshipping, but he likened these denials of secular people about worship to the denials of addicts. "The insidious thing," he said, "is [that] they are unconscious. They are default settings."[19]

Whatever you live for actually owns you. You do not really control yourself. Whatever you live for and love the most controls you.

How can we identify these "default settings" that can so distort our lives, as they did Jonah's? Look at your unanswered prayers and dreams. When God doesn't fulfill them, do you struggle with disappointment but then go on? Or do you examine yourself and learn lessons and make changes and then go on? Or do you feel that "to me death is better than life" (Jonah 4:3)? The difference can tell you if you are dealing with a normal love in your life or an idol.

Once we identify them, how can we change these default settings? The only thing that releases us from the grip of idols is a heart grasp of the radical grace of God. Jonah is on the very brink of understanding this for the first time. In 2:8 he speaks of pagan idolaters and says, "Those clinging to empty idols forfeit the grace that is *theirs*." Literally, he says idolaters forsake *their own grace*. For a moment he understands. He is saying, as it were, "I see now that since salvation is of the Lord, it is only by free grace and mercy alone, and therefore no one is different. The morally 'good' people and the wicked pagans—the grace of God is as much theirs as it is ours! We are all undeserving, but we can all receive it." Had he grasped this idea fully, it would have purged him of the self-righteousness that reasserted itself after Nineveh was spared. It would have demoted his love of country from an ultimate thing to a good thing, and so his disappointment in chapter 4 would not have erupted into suicidal despair.

At the end of chapter 2, it seemed that Jonah was about to make the change from a moralistic identity to a gracious identity. It turns out he is somewhat like the man who needed more than one touch by Jesus (Mark 8:23–25). Most of us are like Jonah. We must have multiple exposures both to our need for God's grace—which usually come through experiences of disappointment and failure—and to the gospel message. To get God's love and Christ's grace down into the motivational principles of our hearts, to the foundational layer of our identities, is a process, and often a slow one.

How can we be freed from our idols, self-salvations, and self-justifications, which are so fragile and subject to circumstances? Only through the grace of God, which cuts us to the quick (Acts 2:37) but lifts us higher than the heavens (Ephesians 1:3–10), grounding our happiness and identity in the unchanging love of the Father. The gospel holds out to us the prospect of a self-worth not *achieved but received*. While we maintain all our identifications with our race, nationality, gender, family, community, and other connections, the most fundamental thing about us is that we are sinners saved by grace. In ourselves we are lost, flawed, and undeserving, but in Christ we are completely accepted and delighted in by the one in the universe we adore the most.

On the one hand, such a received identity sweeps aside our pride and humbles us. How can we feel superior to anyone else if our standing before God is only by grace's riches at Christ's expense? On the other hand, we are absolutely assured of God's endless, unchanging love as we appear in Christ. "There is now no condemnation for those who are in Christ Jesus"

(Romans 8:1). There is no need to inflate our self-image by excluding others.

The Character of Compassion (Jonah 4:4–11)

God did not try to liberate Jonah from his self-righteous identity with only a speech. We must not forget he also sent Jonah difficulties and disappointments. The first time he sent a life-threatening storm. The second time he took away the plant that had been such a comfort to him. Something he loved withered and died. Why did God do it? Because he was being merciful and therefore was doing spiritual surgery on the idols of Jonah's heart. John Newton has an entire hymn about this passage where God blasts this vine, here called a "gourd."

> *I asked the Lord, that I might grow*
> *In faith, and love, and every grace;*
> *Might more of his salvation know;*
> *And seek more earnestly his face . . .*

I hoped that in some favored hour,
At once he'd answer my request;
And by his love's constraining power
Subdue my sins—and give me rest.

Instead of this, he made me feel
The hidden evils of my heart;
And let the angry powers of hell
Assault my soul in every part.

Yea more, with his own hand he seemed
Intent to aggravate my woe;
Crossed all the fair designs I schemed,
Blasted my gourds, and laid me low.

"Lord, why is this," I trembling cried,
"Wilt thou pursue thy worm to death?"
"'Tis in this way," the Lord replied,
"I answer prayer for grace and faith.

These inward trials I employ,
From self, and pride, to set thee free;

> *And break they schemes of earthly joy,*
> *That thou may'st find thy all in me.*"[20]

This remarkable hymn is almost a commentary on the final dialogue between Jonah and God. Jonah, like any prophet of the Lord, certainly wanted to grow in character and wanted God to help him. God seemed, on the contrary, to be pursuing him with disappointment and disaster. God "blasted his gourds," not just the literal one that had given him shade and comfort but also the bigger one, his passion for his nation's prosperity and success, and his biggest one, his pride in his own righteousness.

Why was God sending a deluge of disappointments? "Tis in this way," the Lord replied, in essence: "I am *answering* your prayers for grace and faith. I am only trying to liberate you from the things that enslave you, drive you, and control you. Do you not see that if you loved me supremely, more than anything else, you'd be truly free? Find your all in me."

This call of God to Jonah is a call to us. It is a painful process to find our all in him, but it is the only real path to joy. So let us not feel sorry for ourselves. Jesus trod an infinitely more painful path for "the joy set before him" (Hebrews 12:2)—for the joy of delighting his Father and redeeming us, his brothers and sisters (Hebrews 2:10–15).

The final verses of the book tell us that the mark of those who have been immersed in the grace of God is compassion and love, not contempt, for people who aren't like them. God challenges Jonah for confronting profane, ungodly people without weeping and compassion. Certainly error and evil must be denounced. However, God is both just and loving, and he rebukes Jonah for preaching to the city without loving the city.

We live in a world fragmented into various "media bubbles," in which you hear only news that confirms what you already believe. Anyone who uses the internet and social media or who even watches most news channels today is being daily encouraged in a dozen ways to become like Jonah with regard to "those people over there." Groups demonize and mock other groups. Each region of the country and political party finds reasons to despise the others. Christian believers today are being sucked into this maelstrom as much as if not more than anyone else. The book of Jonah is a shot across the bow. God asks, how can we look at anyone—even those with deeply opposing beliefs and practices—with no compassion?

If your compassion is going to resemble God's, you must abandon a cozy world of self-protection. God's compassion meant he could not stay perched above the circle of the earth and simply feel bad for us. He came down, he took on a human nature, he literally stepped into our shoes and into our condition and problems and walked with us. If you have a friend who's going through a really hard time, don't be too busy to spend time with them. Walk with them through this suffering. Of course you're going to weep. It's going to hurt! That's what God did for you.

WHO TOLD THE STORY?

We are called to be people in mission, to become vulnerable in order to share our faith and love our neighbors. That is what God did in Jesus Christ, and that is what even Jonah eventually did. He went to Nineveh and preached. Yet in his anger, he withdrew. He stayed outside the city in hopes of viewing its demise. Did he fail in the end?

As we have seen, the book of Jonah ends with a cliff-hanger. We are never told how the prophet responded to God's final appeal. I propose, however, that we can make a reasonable guess about how Jonah ultimately responded to God. How do we know Jonah was so recalcitrant, defiant, and clueless? How do we know that he made that unbelievable "I hate the God of love" speech? How do we know about his prayer inside the fish? The only way we could possibly know these things is if Jonah told others. What kind of man would let the world see what a fool he was? Only someone who had become joyfully secure in God's love. Only someone who believed that he was simultaneously sinful but completely accepted. In short, someone who has found in the gospel of grace the very power of God (Romans 1:16).

If it can change Jonah, it can change anyone. It can change you.

ACKNOWLEDGMENTS

Although my wife Kathy is not a co-author of this volume, she has been the main force behind its coming to publication. I preached through the book of Jonah in three sermon series, once in 1981, once in 1991, and once in 2001. Only Kathy heard all of them, and for years she has wanted them put into book form. It is difficult to turn a set of oral presentations, each of which had to stand alone for the listeners assembled that Sunday, into a continuous written narrative that nevertheless draws out the numerous and varied lines of application to contemporary issues and problems. She sent me back to the drawing board more than once, and has worked carefully with the manuscript through every phase of editing.

This is the first of my books to be dedicated to a "historic" figure—the Rev. John Newton. He had been raised in a Christian home, but abandoned religion and became a slave trader, running hard from God. But during a dramatic storm in the Atlantic, he prayed and began a journey toward a vibrant faith. Like Jonah, he went to preach in the great city. Eventually he became a prominent evangelical

Anglican priest in London. Kathy and I have found his pastoral letters to be without peer. Their practical wisdom, theological depth, and grace-centeredness have helped us again and again over the years, sometimes in the very darkest moments.

I want, as usual, to thank those who gave me great places and spaces to work and write, including Ray and Gill Lane of The Fisherbeck Hotel in Ambleside, Cumbria, UK, and Janice Worth of Palm Beach Gardens, Florida, where several years ago I wrote the first drafts of this book. And again I thank David McCormick and Brian Tart whose editorial and literary guidance has been fundamental to all my writing.

NOTES

INTRODUCTION:
Prodigal Prophet

1. One of the most extensive surveys of all of the interpretations of Jonah over the years is found in Yvonne Sherwood, *A Biblical Text and Its Afterlives: The Survival of Jonah in Western Culture* (Cambridge: Cambridge University Press, 2000). Sherwood argues that commentators have tended to use Jonah to further their own beliefs and views. That is certainly true but it is an ironic thesis for Sherwood, who herself uses the book to promote a late-modern agenda, namely, that no one interpretation has more validity than any other. The earliest Christian commentators, such as Jerome and Augustine, saw Jonah as a type of Christ. Many reformers, such as Luther, saw Jonah as a Jew unwilling to reach out to the Gentiles, showing a failure of Israel both to grasp the gospel and to be a witness to the nations. From the Enlightenment onward, a major approach to the story was to critique or defend the plausibility of the story, particularly the fish incident. A more recent avenue of interpretation is literary analysis, in which Jonah is often classified as a satire or comedy. Each of these lines of interpretation makes important points and provides important insights for understanding the text.
2. For an exhaustive case for biblical miracles, see the two-volume work by Craig S. Keener, *Miracles: The Credibility of the New Testament Accounts* (Grand Rapids, MI: Baker Academic, 2011).

3. David W. Baker, T. Desmond Alexander, and Bruce K. Waltke, *Obadiah, Jonah, and Micah: An Introduction and Commentary*, Tyndale Old Testament Commentaries vol. 26 (Downers Grove, IL: InterVarsity Press, 1988), p. 123.

CHAPTER 1:
Running from God

1. The translation of Jonah I use throughout is derived from my own exegetical work and from that of those with greater skill in Hebrew than I. But it is heavily influenced by the insights of Jack M. Sasson, *Jonah: A New Translation with Introduction, Commentary, and Interpretation*, The Anchor Bible (New York: Doubleday, 1990); and Phyllis Trible, *Rhetorical Criticism: Context, Method, and the Book of Jonah* (Philadelphia: Fortress, 1994). All citations of the text of Jonah, therefore, are of my translation. All other Biblical quotes and citations from the rest of the Bible follow the New International Version.

2. Erika Bleibtreu, "Grisly Assyrian Record of Torture and Death," *Biblical Archaeology Review*, January/February 1991, pp. 52–61, quoted in James Bruckner, *The NIV Application Commentary: Jonah, Nahum, Habakkuk, Zephaniah* (Grand Rapids, MI: Zondervan, 2004), p. 28.

3. Bruckner, *NIV Application Commentary*, pp. 28–29.

4. Bruckner assembles three pages of historical records of what he calls the Assyrian empire's "Terror-Mongering," *NIV Application Commentary*, pp. 28–30.

5. Leslie C. Allen, *The Books of Joel, Obadiah, Jonah, and Micah* (Grand Rapids, MI: Wm. B. Eerdmans, 1976), p. 202; Rosemary Nixon, *The Message of Jonah* (Downers Grove, IL: InterVarsity Press, 2003,) pp. 56–58.

6. See Allen, *The Books of Joel*, pp. 204–5.

7. The majority of biblical scholars date the prophecy of Nahum earlier than Jonah. See T. F. Glasson, "The Final Question in

Nahum and Jonah," *Expository Times* 81 (1969), pp. 54–55. Leslie Allen adds that Jonah's hostility to Nineveh is perfectly understandable if we remember "the religious and psychological impact of the old Assyrian capital upon a community that had received the book of Nahum as part of its religious heritage" (Allen, *The Books of Joel*, p. 190).

8. "[A]s in Job, the relevant lesson [of the book of Jonah] is about the incapacity of mortals to understand, let alone to judge, their God." Jack M. Sasson, *Jonah: A New Translation, with Introduction, Commentary, and Interpretation,* The Anchor Bible (New York: Doubleday, 1990), p. 351.

9. For an exposition of this parable, see Timothy Keller, *The Prodigal God: Recovering the Heart of the Christian Faith* (New York: Dutton, 2008). I use the word "prodigal" in its more original meaning of being "recklessly extravagant." While the younger brother is wastefully so with money, the father shows himself to be extravagant with his grace.

10. Flannery O'Connor, *Wise Blood: A Novel* (New York: Farrar, Straus and Giroux, 1990), p. 22. I treat this subject of using religion to avoid God in more depth in chapter 3, "Redefining Sin," in *The Prodigal God*, pp. 34–54.

11. "Jonah effectively views himself as God, turning the true God into an element in a larger equation that Jonah himself wants to control." Daniel C. Timmer, *A Gracious and Compassionate God: Mission, Salvation and Spirituality in the Book of Jonah* (Downers Grove, IL: InterVarsity Press, 2011), p. 144.

12. Timmer points out that because Jonah has already been the "younger brother" and has asked for forgiveness, his relapse into being an elder brother is all the more shocking. "Jonah wants to receive God's grace without being changed by it, and at the same time to snatch it away from those whose lives *are* in fact changed by it." Timmer, *Gracious and Compassionate God*, p. 133.

CHAPTER 2:
The World's Storms

1. Derek Kidner, *Proverbs: An Introduction and Commentary* (Downers Grove, IL: InterVarsity Press, 1964), p. 80.
2. Quoted Genesis 6:6 is from the New Century Version translation of the Bible. Quoted Isaiah 63:9 is from the English Standard Version.

CHAPTER 3:
Who Is My Neighbor?

1. Hugh Martin, "The Prayer of Terror and the Sleep of Sorrow in the Storm," in *A Commentary on Jonah* (Edinburgh: Banner of Truth, 1958), p. 91.
2. Leslie C. Allen, *The Books of Joel* (Grand Rapids, MI: Wm. B. Eerdmans, 1976), p. 207.
3. Allen, *The Books of Joel*, pp. 207–8.
4. Phyllis Trible, "Jonah," in *The New Interpreter's Bible, Volume Seven: Introduction to Apocalyptic Literature, Daniel, The Twelve Prophets* (Nashville: Abingdon Press, 1996) p. 498. See also Jack M. Sasson, *Jonah: A New Translation with Introduction, Commentary, and Interpretation*, The Anchor Bible (New York: Doubleday, 1990), pp. 110–11.
5. Martin, "The World Rebuking the Church," *Commentary on Jonah*, pp. 94–107.
6. Jacques Ellul, *The Judgment of Jonah* (Grand Rapids, MI: Eerdmans, 1971), p. 29.
7. Francis Schaeffer, *The Church Before the Watching World* (Downers Grove, IL: InterVarsity Press, 1971).
8. Phyllis Trible, "Jonah," in *The New Interpreter's Bible, Volume Seven*, p. 502.
9. In these verses James is referring to mercy on poor believers (see verse 15: "a brother or a sister"). So in this instance James is

saying that the sign that we are saved by grace is that we take practical action to alleviate the suffering of the poor in the Christian community. This text needs to be put alongside Galatians 6:10, where Paul tells Christians to "do good" (give practical help) "to all people, especially to those who belong to the family of believers." In other words, compassion for the economic and material needs of all people, but especially of others within the church, is one of the marks of true faith.

CHAPTER 4:
Embracing the Other

1. Verse 8 uses the Hebrew word *melaka*, translated here as "mission" but sometimes merely as "job." Jack Sasson gives the evidence for why it is best to understand that the sailors are asking Jonah not simply about his career but rather for his mission and purpose on the voyage and in life. Jack M. Sasson, *Jonah: A New Translation, with Introduction, Commentary, and Interpretation*, The Anchor Bible (New York: Doubleday, 1990), p. 114.

2. For more on this subject, see Timothy Keller, *Counterfeit Gods: The Empty Promises of Sex, Money, and Power and the Only Hope That Matters* (New York: Dutton, 2009).

3. See the biblical-theological study by Richard Lints, *Identity and Idolatry: The Image of God and Its Inversion* (Downers Grove, IL: InterVarsity Press, 2015). The title of this section of the chapter comes from Lints's important volume. Also see Thomas C. Oden, *Two Worlds: Notes on the Death of Modernity in America and Russia* (Downers Grove, IL: InterVarsity Press, 1992), chapter 6.

4. Daniel C. Timmer, *A Gracious and Compassionate God: Mission, Salvation, and Spirituality in the Book of Jonah* (Downers Grove, IL: InterVarsity Press, 2011), p. 70.

5. Miroslav Volf outlines four forms of exclusion—attacking, assimilating, dominating, and abandoning. I have combined

attacking and dominating under the category "removing." See Miroslav Volf, *Exclusion and Embrace: A Theological Exploration of Identity, Otherness, and Reconciliation* (Nashville: Abingdon Press, 1996), pp. 74–78.

CHAPTER 5:
The Pattern of Love

1. Leslie C. Allen, *The Books of Joel* (Grand Rapids, MI: Wm. B. Eerdmans, 1976), p. 211.

2. In the two places in the gospel that Jesus speaks of "the sign of Jonah," skeptics demanded that Jesus produce miraculous evidence to establish his claims. They wanted a "sign"—powerful evidence that God was with him. Of course they had seen him do miracles, but many people seemed to be able to work miracles. They wanted a decisive sign that showed he was who he said he was. Jesus responded that no sign would be given "except the sign of Jonah." Both Matthew (12:38–42) and Luke (11:29–32) record this. But what was this "sign"?

Matthew refers to Jonah's "death" and "resurrection" ("three days and nights in the belly of a huge fish") with Jesus's death and resurrection ("three days in the belly of the earth"). Luke, however, omits any reference to the three days in the fish and in the earth. In Luke Jesus says that the sign of Jonah was his preaching of repentance to Nineveh. Some interpreters, focusing exclusively on the Matthew text, believe that the resurrection of Christ, the ultimate miracle, is the "sign" in that it will prove to all that Jesus is who he said he is. But Luke was able to talk about the sign of Jonah without mentioning the resurrection.

Other interpreters, focusing exclusively on Luke, think Jesus meant that he was not going to produce any miraculous signs at all; he was just going to preach the gospel. But as Joachim Jeremias points out, "it is highly unusual to describe the preaching of repentance as a *semeion*, since a sign consists, not in what men do, but in the 'intervention of the power of God.'" Joachim Jeremias, "Ionas," in *Theological Dictionary of the New Testament*, edited by G. Kittell and G. Friedrich (Grand Rapids, MI: Wm. B. Eerdmans, 1976), p. 409, quoted in Baker, Alexander, and Waltke, *Obadiah, Jonah, and Micah,* p. 92.

T. D. Alexander concludes that Jesus's reference to Jonah makes the most sense if we combine the ideas. (Baker, Alexander, and Walke, *Obadiah, Jonah, and Micah*, p. 94). Just as Jonah was cast into the water to save the sailors from the wrath of God, so Jesus would be cast into death to bear all the punishment our sins deserve, to save us. And it is only if we repent in the light of Christ's death and resurrection in our place that we find God and receive his new life. If we repent thinking that we can attract God's pity through our contrition and efforts at purification, it will be for naught. There is the sign of Jonah—to repent and believe, not as ways to win God's approval but resting in Jesus's permanent, full procurement of the love and approval of God, all through his finished work.

3. Jacques Ellul, *The Judgment of Jonah*, (Grand Rapids, MI: Eerdmans, 1971), pp. 36–38.

4. See Albert L. Lukaszewski, "Prepositions," in *The Lexham Syntactic Greek New Testament Glossary* (Bellingham, WA: Lexham Press, 2007), p. 382. See also William L. Lane, *The Gospel of Mark* (Grand Rapids, MI: Eerdmans, 1974), p. 384.

5. P. P. Bliss, "'Man of Sorrows,' What a Name" (hymn), 1875.

6. Allen, *The Books of Joel*, p. 212.

7. The Greek word *hilasmos*—rendered "propitiation" in the King James Bible and the English Standard Version—has been a source of controversy. Outside the Bible the Greek word in common ancient usage meant an offering made to placate the wrath of a god who had been offended. However, in the late nineteenth and early twentieth centuries, scholars such as B. F.

Westcott and C. H. Dodd argued that, within the New Testament, the word did not refer to God and his wrath but to us and our sin. They taught that the word instead meant "expiation," that is, our sins are removed as obstacles to our relationship with God. We are forgiven; we are declared not guilty. These scholars denied that the word meant "to placate or satisfy the wrath of God." However, Leon Morris (*The Apostolic Preaching of the Cross*, London: Tyndale, 1965) and David Hill (*Greek Words and Hebrew Meanings*, Cambridge: Cambridge University Press, 1967) have strongly and decisively challenged this view. They show that the *hilasmos* word group in the Bible does have the same meaning as it had in outside Greek literature. They also make the case that expiation and propitiation must happen together. If an offender has sinned against someone, then the offended party's rightful anger and desire for justice pose a barrier in the relationship until the offender admits the wrong and pays the debt to justice. So to remove the sin as a barrier and to change the offended party's attitude to the offender are two sides of the same action. See also R. R. Nicole, "C. H. Dodd and the Doctrine of Propitiation," *Westminster Theological Journal* 17 (1954–55): 117–57.

8. For example, see Mark Baer, "The Passion of Anger Can Be Used in a Constructive Manner," *Psychology Today*, April 12, 2017, www.psychologytoday.com/intl/blog/empathy-and-relationships/201704/the-passion-anger-can-be-used-in-constructive-manner. This article makes some obvious points: (a) that Christian teaching, expressed by Thomas Aquinas, is that anger per se, a desire to deal with injustice and wrong, can be good if not accompanied by pride and arrogance rather than humility and if not expressing a swollen overdesire for vengeance; and (b) that anyone with a love of justice and a love for people who are exploited will experience anger as a resource for doing justice.

9. Daniel C. Timmer, *A Gracious and Compassionate God: Mission, Salvation, and Spirituality in the Book of Jonah* (Downers Grove, IL: InterVarsity Press, 2011), p. 75.

10. James Montgomery Boice, *The Minor Prophets: An Expositional Commentary*, vol. 1, *Hosea–Jonah* (Grand Rapids, MI: Baker, 1983), p. 280.

CHAPTER 6

Running from Grace

1. Daniel C. Timmer, *A Gracious and Compassionate God: Mission, Salvation, and Spirituality in the Book of Jonah* (Downers Grove, IL: InterVarsity Press, 2011), p. 77.

2. Peter C. Craigie, *Twelve Prophets*, vol. 1, *Hosea, Joel, Amos, Obadiah, Jonah* (Louisville, KY: Westminster John Knox Press, 1984), p. 227.

3. Marta Bousells, "J. K. Rowling's Life Advice," *Guardian*, March 30, 2015. The commencement address was published as *Very Good Lives: The Fringe Benefits of Failure and the Importance of Imagination* (New York: Little, Brown, 2008).

4. Jack M. Sasson, *Jonah: A New Translation, with Introduction, Commentary, and Interpretation*, The Anchor Bible (New York: Doubleday, 1990), p. 157.

5. J. I. Packer, *Knowing God* (Downers Grove, IL: InterVarsity Press, 1973), p. 117.

6. Philip Rieff, *The Triumph of the Therapeutic: The Uses of Faith After Freud* (Chicago: University of Chicago Press, 1966).

7. Packer, *Knowing God*, pp. 118–19.

8. Augustus Toplady, "Rock of Ages" (hymn), quoted in Packer, *Knowing God*, p. 119.

9. Jacques Ellul, *The Judgment of Jonah* (Grand Rapids, MI: Eerdmans, 1971), pp. 48–49. Ellul writes: "Jonah has not been answered if we take the answer to be rescue from the belly of the fish. . . . But he has been answered if we take the answer to

be adoption under the care of God who takes on the totality of our sufferings, dramas, and situations. He is answered because grace does not fail in any way. . . . Events have taken place without any indication of a favorable intervention, only signs of judgment. . . . But simply in the very fact that he has been able to repent, to condemn himself, to recognize the sentence of the just judge [and see the atoning sacrifice in the temple], he has reason enough to say, 'Thou has delivered me.' It is here indeed that the great decision is taken."

10. James Montgomery Boice, *The Minor Prophets: An Expositional Commentary*, vol. 1, *Hosea–Jonah* (Grand Rapids, MI: Baker, 1983), p. 288.

11. Kevin J. Youngblood, *Jonah: Exegetical Commentary on the Old Testament* (Grand Rapids, MI: Zondervan, 2013), p. 114.

CHAPTER 7:
Doing Justice, Preaching Wrath

1. Daniel C. Timmer, *A Gracious and Compassionate God: Mission, Salvation, and Spirituality in the Book of Jonah* (Downers Grove, IL: InterVarsity Press, 2011), p. 94.

2. Jacques Ellul, *The Judgment of Jonah* (Grand Rapids, MI: Eerdmans, 1971), p. 97.

3. See Thomas S. Kidd, "The North Korean Revival of 1907," The Gospel Coalition, May 2, 2017, www.thegospelcoalition.org /blogs/evangelical-history/the-north-korean-revival-of-1907/; and Young-Hoon Lee, "Korean Pentecost: The Great Revival of 1907," *Asian Journal of Pentecostal Studies* 4, no. 1 (2001): 73–83.

4. See William N. Blair and Bruce F. Hunt, *The Korean Pentecost and the Sufferings That Followed* (Edinburgh: Banner of Truth, 1977).

5. P. Trible writes: "The narrator reports the radical theological turning of the city, though not its conversion to Yahwism." P. Trible, "Jonah," in *The New Interpreter's Bible*, vol. 7 (Nashville: Abingdon Press, 1996), p. 513.

6. Leslie C. Allen, *The Books of Joel* (Grand Rapids, MI: Wm. B. Eerdmans, 1976), p. 225.

7. Christopher J. H. Wright, *The Mission of God: Unlocking the Bible's Grand Narrative* (Downers Grove, IL: InterVarsity Press, 2013), p. 185.

8. See Timmer, *Gracious and Compassionate God*, p. 41.

9. Old Testament scholar H. L. Ellison concludes that modern-day readers should learn from Jonah that Christians are called to go to the cities and places of great need and become involved in "social services" that are "not simply . . . a means to an evangelistic end." See R. E. Clements, "The Purpose of the Book of Jonah," *Supplement to Vetus Testamentum* 28 (1975): 18, quoted in Baker, Alexander, and Waltke, *Obadiah, Jonah, and Micah*, p. 86.

10. See Trible, "Jonah," p. 516, where she speaks of the repentance of Nineveh across the classes as "addressing systemic concerns," as an encouragement for those who desire "corporate and social" healing for cities.

11. Ellul, *The Judgment of Jonah*, p. 88.

12. The translation is the English Standard Version.

13. Alec Motyer, *The Prophecy of Isaiah: An Introduction and Commentary* (Downers Grove, IL: InterVarsity Press, 1994), p. 109.

14. Martin Luther King Jr., "Letter from a Birmingham Jail," April 16, 1963, www.africa.upenn.edu/Articles_Gen/Letter _Birmingham.html.

15. Martin Luther King Jr., "I Have a Dream" (speech, Washington DC, August 28, 1963), www.americanrhetoric.com/speeches /mlkihaveadream.htm.

CHAPTER 8:
Heart Storms

1. Peter C. Craigie, *Twelve Prophets*, vol. 1, *Hosea, Joel, Amos, Obadiah, Jonah* (Louisville, KY: Westminster John Knox Press, 1984), p. 233.

2. Jacques Ellul, *The Judgment of Jonah* (Grand Rapids, MI: Eerdmans, 1971), p. 74.
3. Ibid.
4. Ibid.
5. Ellul, *The Judgment of Jonah*, p. 75.
6. Ibid.
7. Jonathan Haidt, *The Righteous Mind: Why Good People Are Divided by Politics and Religion* (New York: Vintage, 2013), pp. xix, xx.

CHAPTER 9:
The Character of Compassion

1. Jacques Ellul, *The Judgment of Jonah* (Grand Rapids, MI: Eerdmans, 1971), pp. 72–73.
2. Daniel C. Timmer, *A Gracious and Compassionate God: Mission, Salvation, and Spirituality in the Book of Jonah* (Downers Grove, IL: InterVarsity Press, 2011), p. 127.
3. Leslie C. Allen, *The Books of Joel* (Grand Rapids, MI: Wm. B. Eerdmans, 1976), p. 232.
4. See Massimo Pigliucci, "Stoicism," Internet Encyclopedia of Philosophy, no date, www.iep.utm.edu/stoicism.
5. James Bruckner, *The NIV Application Commentary: Jonah, Nahum, Habakkuk, Zephaniah* (Grand Rapids, MI: Zondervan, 2004), p. 116 and 7n.
6. The translation is the New Century Version. The Hebrew word used here is to grieve to the point of pain and anguish.
7. Even Christian theologians must wrestle with how this language fits with the idea of God's "aseity." See Herman Bavinck, *Reformed Dogmatics*, vol. 2 (Grand Rapids, MI: Baker Books, 2004), pp. 149–53. That is a technical word that describes the historical Christian belief that God is not just one more object in the universe, but is the upholder of all existence. He is dependent on nothing and no one—everything is completely dependent on

him. We cannot read the various places that speak of God's compassion and even the pain in his heart that his love for us causes (Genesis 6:6; Hosea 11:8–11) without asking whether God is changing or becoming in some way dependent on us. We must not in any way move toward an "open theism" position that sees God as evolving or dependent on his creation. Rather, in his freedom and sovereignty he voluntarily allows his love for us to cause him grief in ways analogous (though not identical) to the ways love causes us pain and sorrow. See also note 9 in this chapter.

8. John Calvin, *Commentaries of the Twelve Minor Prophets*, vol. 3, translated by J. Owen (Grand Rapids, MI: Baker Books, 1979), p. 141.

9. See "The Emotional Life of Our Lord," in B. B. Warfield *Person and Work of Christ*, ed. Samuel G. Craig (Philadelphia: The Presbyterian and Reformed Publishing Company, 1950), pp. 93–145.

10. Miroslav Volf, *Exclusion and Embrace: A Theological Exploration of Identity, Otherness, and Reconciliation* (Nashville: Abingdon Press, 1996), pp. 303–4.

11. See James E. Dolezal, *All That Is in God: Evangelical Theology and the Challenge of Classical Christian Theism* (Grand Rapids, MI: Reformation Heritage Books, 2017). This book expounds the historical doctrine of the "simplicity" of God, namely, that he does not consist of parts, but that all that is in God is a perfect unity. Nevertheless, this right understanding of the simplicity of God must not be made to flatten or trivialize the biblical descriptions of God's heart attachment to and sorrow over his creation, nor to undermine the necessity and reality of atonement if God is going to pardon us. See Joseph Minich, "A Review of James Dolezal's *All That Is in God*," The Calvinist International, August 31, 2017, https://calvinistinternational.com/2017/08/31/review-james-dolezals-god.

12. This interpretation of Exodus 33–34 and the argument that the cross shows us "all the goodness" are indebted to D. M. Lloyd-Jones, "The Goodness of God Made Manifest," in *Revival* (Wheaton, IL: Crossway Books. 1987), pp. 225–36.

13. Sinclair B. Ferguson, *Man Overboard: Study of the Life of Jonah* (Wheaton, IL: Tyndale House, 1981), p. 118.

CHAPTER 10:
Our Relationship to God's Word

1. For an exposition and explanation of this important idea, see Sinclair Ferguson, *The Whole Christ: Legalism, Antinomianism, and Gospel Assurance—Why the Marrow Controversy Still Matters* (Wheaton, IL: Crossway Books, 2016), pp. 68–82.

2. From the King James Version.

3. See Nicholas Kristof, "A Little Respect for Dr. Foster," *New York Times*, March 28, 2015, www.nytimes.com/2015/03/29/opinion /sunday/nicholas-kristof-a-little-respect-for-dr-foster.html.

4. John Newton, "Letter XVI *Temptation*," *Letters of John Newton* (Edinburgh: Banner of Truth Trust, 1960), pp. 94–95. All of "Letter XVI *Temptation*" is relevant.

5. Newton, "Letter XVI *Temptation*," p. 94.

6. While it is right to believe that God works good things in our lives through suffering, we must not breezily respond to people who are in pain by just quoting Bible verses about God's purposes in trials. When we meet people who are going through life storms, we must not try to be "minimizers, teachers, or solvers," three unhelpful responses we can make to people going through suffering. Minimizers may say things like "Things could be worse— you could have been born in poverty in some foreign country." Teachers may say, "God is teaching you things—so look for the lessons." Solvers will talk like this: "If you just keep your chin up and do X, Y, and Z, you can come through this." (These three

unhelpful responses are laid out by Kate Bowler in "What to Say When You Meet the Angel of Death at a Party," *New York Times*, January 26, 2018.) A better way to help sufferers is often to simply weep with them and love them, as Jesus did with Mary when her brother Lazarus died (John 11:32–36).

7. John Newton, "I Will Trust, and Not Be Afraid," in "Olney Hymns," in John Newton and Richard Cecil, *The Works of John Newton*, vol. 3 (London: Hamilton, Adams, 1824), p. 609.

8. John Stott, *The Cross of Christ* (Downers Grove, IL: InterVarsity Press, 1986), p. 276.

9. Stott, *Cross of Christ*, p. 292.

10. Jennifer Senior, *All Joy and No Fun: The Paradox of Modern Parenthood* (New York: HarperCollins, 2014), p. 44.

11. Donald B. Kraybill et al., *Amish Grace: How Forgiveness Transcended Tragedy* (San Francisco: Josey-Bass, 2007), pp. 114, 138.

12. Ernest Gordon, *Through the Valley of the Kwai* (New York: Harper, 1962), pp. 104–5.

13. J. K. Rowling, *Harry Potter and the Sorcerer's Stone* (New York: Scholastic Press, 1999), p. 299.

14. Stott, *Cross of Christ*, p. 159.

15. George Buttrick, quoted in Stott, *Cross of Christ*, p. 158.

16. Stott, *Cross of Christ*, pp. 159–60.

CHAPTER 11:
Our Relationship to God's World

1. To Jews, Samaritans were "socio-religious outcasts." Joel B. Green, *The Gospel of Luke*, The New International Commentary on the New Testament (Grand Rapids, MI: Wm. B. Eerdmans, 1997), p. 431.

2. Green, *Gospel of Luke*, p. 432.

3. An accessible treatment of this doctrine is Anthony A. Hoekema, *Created in God's Image* (Grand Rapids, MI: Wm. B. Eerdmans, 1994).

4. John Calvin, *Institutes of the Christian Religion*, vol. 1, edited by John T. McNeill, translated by Ford Lewis Battles, The Library of Christian Classics (Louisville, KY: Westminster John Knox Press, 2011), pp. 696–97. Italics are mine.

5. Calvin, *Institutes of the Christian Religion*, p. 698.

6. An important, scholarly work exploring how Christians and local churches can work for the common good of neighborhoods and cities is Luke Bretherton, *Resurrecting Democracy: Faith, Citizenship, and the Politics of a Common Life* (Cambridge: Cambridge University Press, 2014). Bretherton addresses the question "How do we build a common life in places characterized by deep religious and cultural diversity?" He calls for churches and Christians to engage in "broad-based community organizing," in which believers come together with people of deeply different beliefs, identify ways to improve life for all in their locale, and work together for change.

7. It is important to note that believers can serve in politics and government faithfully without the obligation to turn the government into a Christian state. Daniel calls a pagan king to act justly toward the poor and the oppressed (Daniel 4:27), and Amos 1–2 shows God holding pagan nations accountable for their behavior. They are not being called to acknowledge God as Lord; still less are governments being held to a full Christian ethical standard. But they are being held to something like the golden rule. That golden-rule level of justice and fairness in society is something that Christian ministers can call pagan governments to honor, as Amos and Daniel did.

8. In ancient Israel it was the state's role to promote true religion and punish heresy. Thus Israel was a theocratic state. In the New Testament, however, Jesus tells us to "give back to Caesar what is Caesar's, and to God what is God's" (Matthew 22:21). Many (including me) see this as a change in the relationship of the church to the state to one of "nonestablishment."

This does not mean that any government can really be completely "religiously neutral." All political orders are based on some vision of moral good. A government might be committed to a post-Enlightenment belief in absolute individual freedom or instead a traditional one of family and clan solidarity. It will embrace one of the many particular definitions of "justice," whether it be the utilitarianism of John Stuart Mill or individual-rights justice or the virtue ethics of Aristotle. But none of these views is empirically provable. They are faith-based moral visions grounded in beliefs about human nature and purpose. That means that Christians have every right, as individual citizens, to seek social policies based on their own beliefs, just as all other citizens inevitably will be doing.

That is not, however, the same as seeking to establish one religion or denomination as the official church of the state. In general, then, the church should produce individual Christians—"the church scattered"—who engage in political action, but the institutional "gathered" church and its leaders should not be aligned with particular political parties and leaders. See Daniel Strange, "Evangelical Public Theology: What on Earth? Why on Earth? How on Earth?" in *A Higher Throne: Evangelical Public Theology*, edited by Chris Green (London: InterVarsity Press, 2008), pp. 58–61. This is a sympathetic but critical review of Abraham Kuyper's teaching that the "organic" church of individual Christians should do cultural transformation but that the "institutional" church should not. For a lengthier critical, but ultimately sympathetic case for Abraham Kuyper's public theology (with lots of appreciation for pessimists like MacIntyre and Hauerwas) see James K. A. Smith, *Awaiting the King: Reforming Public Theology* (Grand Rapids, MI: Baker Academic, 2017).

9. The gospel itself undermines extreme partisanship because of the doctrine of sin. It tells Christians that the evil ruining human life on this planet resides in every single human heart, including

theirs. Each side of the political spectrum has a tendency to argue that the evil we suffer is mainly from certain classes of people—the wealthy and powerful people and races or the poor and the immigrant. But the Christian believes in the doctrine of "total depravity," namely, that no race, class, or gender is more sinful and depraved than any other. Yes, a group with more power can do more damage with their sin, but Christians are forbidden to think that a different class of person with power is intrinsically less prone to sin and exploitation.

This teaching of total depravity undermines partisanship also because it prevents us from thinking that either the "invisible hand" of capital markets or the power of government is more intrinsically trustworthy as a guide for the allocation of material resources. The extreme Left is far more suspicious of capitalism than of the state, and the extreme Right tends to be the opposite. But the "market" and the "state" are simply human beings. Human beings are intrinsically self-centered, and they will find ways to use the power they have to privilege themselves.

It is true that secular political systems of the Right and Left make idols out of individual choice or the state or capitalism, and this leads to policies that favor certain classes over others, undermining the common good. Believers should not, however, think that somehow a Christian political party would necessarily be free from the same problems. The Christian doctrine of sin should lead Christians to mistrust even themselves, since our sinful hearts are perfectly capable of finding justification for abuses of power within a doctrinally orthodox framework.

10. See Sean Michael Lucas, "Owning Our Past: The Spirituality of the Church in History, Failure, and Hope," *Reformed Faith and Practice: The Journal of Reformed Theological Seminary* 1, no. 1 (May 2016), https://journal.rts.edu/article/owning-our-past -the-spirituality-of-the-church-in-history-failure-and-hope.

Lucas discusses the Presbyterian Church's Westminster Confession of Faith 31:4: "Synods and councils are to handle, or conclude nothing, but that which is ecclesiastical: and are not to intermeddle with civil affairs which concern the commonwealth, unless by way of humble petition in cases extraordinary." Many have argued that this forbids the church to speak officially about any social issues, and southern Presbyterians in the 1840s and 1850s invoked this part of the confession against abolitionists who insisted that the church speak out against slavery. Lucas counterargues convincingly that this does not mean that the church cannot speak corporately about issues of race, sex, and poverty, all of which have social implications, since the Bible itself addresses these subjects. He aims to retain, however, the great restraint that the Westminster Confession wants the church to exercise about involvement in electoral politics.

11. This means that ministers and other church leaders ought to exercise great caution in speaking publicly to current political issues, because even if they try to speak as "private citizens," they will unavoidably be seen as speaking officially for the institutional church and thereby claiming that their particular view is the biblical or Christian political position. Some years ago in a private conversation, I was asked what I thought about the Israeli-Palestinian conflict in the Middle East. An agenda was presented to me for a way forward, a possible resolution. After considering the proposal, I said it sounded quite good to me. Then I was asked if I would sign a public petition calling for all parties to adopt this approach. While I was honored to be asked, I declined immediately. I knew the reason I was being asked to sign it was because I was the pastor of a large church and therefore I would be seen as representing a lot of people. But I knew that this particular political solution, though in my view a wise one, was not one dictated by

Scripture. The Christians in my church were free, then, in their consciences to believe otherwise about this issue, and I knew that many did. They would not feel it would be fair for me to sign the petition as if I represented the views of the entire congregation. As a minister whose job it is to preach the Bible to a church, my signature would be read as saying, "This is the Christian, biblical political position on this issue." It wouldn't matter if I protested that I was signing only as a private citizen. I wouldn't have been viewed or heard that way. I would have been tying the gospel and the faith to one debatable political program. Christian ministers and leaders, then, should instruct and encourage believers to be politically active, seeking to be "salt" and "light" (Matthew 5:13–16), using their biblically shaped wisdom to seek the common good. But as representatives of the institutional church, they should not press partisan political agendas.

12. See Craig Blomberg, *Neither Poverty nor Riches: A Biblical Theology of Possessions* (Leicester, UK: Apollos, 1999). Biblical scholar Craig Blomberg examines the biblical data on wealth and economics. He looks at the Mosaic laws, including (a) the Sabbath-year laws that all indentured servants would go free every seven years, whether they had paid off their debts or not; (b) the gleaning laws that limited profit taking by landowners; and (c) the Jubilee, in which land that had been lost in fair business dealing returned to its original owners every fifty years. Blomberg concludes that the rules for the use of wealth and property challenge all major contemporary economic models. They are incompatible with either socialism or democratic capitalism. The Bible "suggests a sharp critique of (1) statism that disregards the precious treasure of personal rootage, and (2) the untrammeled individualism that secures individuals at the expense of community" (p. 46). The Bible teaches "the depersonalization of *both* market forces *and* state-run societies" (p. 83).

13. See James Mumford, "Package Deal Ethics," *Hedgehog Review* 19, no. 3 (Autumn 2017), also available at www.jamesmumford .co.uk/package-deal-ethics-2.

14. See Larry Hurtado, *Destroyer of the Gods: Early Christian Distinctiveness in the Roman World* (Waco, TX: Baylor University Press, 2016). Hurtado points out that the early church was committed to a unique "social project." It stressed (a) multiethnicity and equality between the races, (b) strong concern for the poor, (c) forgiveness and nonretaliation, (d) prohibition of abortion and infanticide, and (e) a sex ethic that prohibited all sex outside of marriage between a man and a woman. As some have pointed out, the first two characteristics sound "Democrat" and the last two sound "Republican," but the third trait— nonretaliation—doesn't sound like either party!

15. Some reading this in 2018–19 will think of evangelicals and Republicans. But this happens across the spectrum. For another example of the pressure of today's political "package deals" when it comes to African American Christians, see Justin E. Giboney, "Oddly, Neither Political Party Reflects the Values of Black Voters," *The Hill*, May 30, 2018, http://thehill.com/opinion/civil-rights/389491-oddly-neither-political-party-reflects -the-values-of-black-voters. Both African American Christians and Catholic social teaching combine "liberal" values in the areas of labor, race, and economics and "conservative" values in the areas of sex, gender, and abortion.

16. Ernest W. Shurtleff, "Lead On, O King Eternal, the Day of March Has Come" (hymn), 1887.

17. Miroslav Volf, *Exclusion and Embrace: A Theological Exploration of Identity, Otherness, and Reconciliation* (Nashville: Abingdon Press, 1996), pp. 74–78.

18. See Jonathan Haidt, "The Age of Outrage: What the Current Political Climate Is Doing to Our Country and Our Universities," *City Journal*, December 17, 2017, www.city-journal.org /html/age-outrage-15608.html.

19. Paul Gilroy, "Diaspora and Detours of Identity," in *Identity and Difference*, edited by K. Woodward (London: Sage/Open University, 1997), p. 302.
20. Volf, *Exclusion and Embrace*, p. 78.
21. Volf, *Exclusion and Embrace*, pp. 63–64.
22. C. S. Lewis, *The Voyage of the Dawn Treader* (New York: Harper Trophy, 2000), p. 110.
23. Volf, *Exclusion and Embrace*, pp. 40, 49.
24. See Larry Hurtado, "A Different Identity," in *Destroyer of the Gods*, pp. 77–104.
25. J. R. R. Tolkien, *The Fellowship of the Ring*, 50th anniversary ed. (New York: Houghton Mifflin, 2004), p. 442.
26. We should not think that the model of the incarnation and the unique Christian identity are the only resources that Christians have for becoming agents of peacemaking and bridge building in a pluralistic society. Here are two others:

    (1) Our doctrine of history undermines both the nostalgia and the utopianism that can lead to extreme political views. Progressives look at the past as filled with darkness and evil and believe our only hope is in a future society we can achieve through politics. On the other hand, conservatives often look back to past "golden eras" and see the present and future as flawed and bleak. But St. Augustine's great work *The City of God* shows the biblical view of history, namely, that the past, present, and future were all filled with human evil and God's sustaining grace, that we can work for a more just society now with both realism and hope, knowing that we will never achieve it until Christ's return. This prevents Christians from either romanticizing the past as conservatives tend to do or putting hopes in utopian political projects as liberals tend to do.

    (2) Our doctrine of salvation by grace alone undermines perhaps the basic human barrier to peaceful, cooperative relation-

ships. Social psychologist Jonathan Haidt has said: "To live virtuously as individuals and societies, we must understand how our minds are built. We must find ways to overcome our natural self-righteousness." Jonathan Haidt, "The Psychology of Self-righteousness" (interview with Krista Tippett), *On Being*, October 19, 2017, https://onbeing.org/programs/jonathan -haidt-the-psychology-of-self-righteousness-oct2017/. It is not being righteous but being self-righteous that leads to constant polarization and alienation within our multicultural, pluralistic societies. One can disagree and critique strongly without de-meaning, demonizing, and dehumanizing the opposing view in both tone and language, but self-righteousness engages in these routinely. John Inazu, in *Confident Pluralism: Surviving and Thriving Through Deep Difference* (Chicago: University of Chicago Press, 2016), argues that we cannot have a peaceful, thriving, pluralistic society, with cooperation among people of deeply different beliefs, unless people speak using the qualities of *tolerance* (treating others with respect and dignity even when we find their views appalling), *humility* (recognizing the limits of what we can prove to them, realizing our beliefs are not self-evident to all), and *patience* (being willing to stick with people, in hope, over the long run). These three traits result in: (a) slowness to attribute bad motives, (b) slowness to think we've figured the other person out, (c) unwillingness to attribute to them a view that they do not hold, even if we think it is an implication of their other views, and (d) refraining from cri-tiquing them until we can first represent their views in ways so compelling that they could not say it better themselves. All of these attitudes and skills are, arguably, becoming less and less prevalent among us. The doctrine of salvation by grace alone means that all human beings are equally lost, unable to save themselves, and saved only by sheer grace. That gives powerful resources for producing tolerance, humility, and patience in

Christians. When we speak to a person who is a Hindu or an atheist, we have no reason to feel superior. We are not saved because we are wiser or more moral but because of grace alone. Even if Christians may have the truth, the remaining sin in our hearts keeps us from ever being as good as our right doctrine should make us.

27. Associated Press, "Dutch Call for End to Religious Violence," *NBC News*, November 9, 2004, www.nbcnews.com/id/6446342 /ns/world_news-europe/t/dutch-call-end-religious-violence /#.Wm9sq5M-dmA.

28. Matthew Kaemingk, *Christian Hospitality and Muslim Immigration in an Age of Fear* (Grand Rapids, MI: Eerdmans, 2018), p. 25. Thanks to Derek Rishmawy for pointing out this great example.

29. Ibid.

30. Kaemingk, *Christian Hospitality and Muslim Immigration*, p. 26.

31. United Nations, "The World's Cities in 2016" (data booklet), no date, www.un.org/en/development/desa/population/publi cations/pdf/urbanization/the_worlds_cities_in_2016_data _booklet.pdf.

32. "Cities in Numbers: How Patterns of Urban Growth Change the World," *Guardian*, November 23, 2015, www.theguardian .com/cities/2015/nov/23/cities-in-numbers-how-patterns -of-urban-growth-change-the-world.

33. Howard Peskett and Vinoth Ramachandra, "Jonah 1–4," in *The Message of Mission: The Glory of Christ in All Time and Space* (Downers Grove, IL: InterVarsity Press, 2003), p. 136.

34. Nevertheless, the move of people, wealth, and power away from the countryside and into the great cities has left rural communities in great need. There is far more drug addiction, poverty, transience, and other social problems in these areas than there was a generation ago. Ministry in these areas requires

new skills and resources. There is a great need for many new churches and for the renewal of innumerable historic churches in those places.

35. Peskett and Ramachandra, "Jonah 1–4," p. 136.

36. Tremper Longman III, *The NIV Application Commentary: Daniel* (Grand Rapids, MI: Zondervan, 1999), pp. 47–48.

37. C. S. Lewis, *The Abolition of Man* (New York: MacMillan, 1947), p. 35.

38. Charles Taylor, *Sources of the Self: The Making of the Modern Identity* (Cambridge, MA: Harvard University Press, 1989), p. 89, speaking about John Rawls's widely accepted theory of moral value. See also pp. 342, 464, 510.

39. George Scialabba, "Charles Taylor's *Sources of the Self: The Making of the Modern Identity*: A Review," *Dissent*, September 1, 1990, http://georgescialabba.net/mtgs/1990/09/sources-of-the-self-the-making.html.

40. Scialabba, "Charles Taylor's *Sources of the Self*."

CHAPTER 12:
Our Relationship to God's Grace

1. Martin Luther, "An Introduction to St. Paul's Letter to the Romans," in *Dr. Martin Luther's vermischte deutsche Schriften*, edited by Johann K. Irmischer, vol. 63 (Erlangen, Germany: Heyder and Zimmer, 1854), pp. 124–25.

2. See "Cheap Grace" in Dietrich Bonhoeffer, *The Cost of Discipleship* (New York: Touchstone, 1995), pp. 43–56.

3. Sigmund Freud attributes this to Heinrich Heine in his *The Joke and Its Relation to the Unconscious* (New York: Penguin, 2003), p. 109.

4. J. I. Packer, *Knowing God* (Downers Grove, IL: InterVarsity Press, 1973), p. 124.

5. Cited in Arnold Dallimore, *George Whitefield: The Life and Times of the Great Evangelist of the Eighteenth Century Revival* (Edinburgh: Banner of Truth, 1970), p. 183.

6. Charles Wesley, "Amazing Love" (hymn), 1738.

7. Bryan D. Estelle, *Salvation Through Judgment and Mercy: The Gospel According to Jonah* (Phillipsburg, NJ: Presbyterian and Reformed Publishing, 2005), pp. 82–83.

8. Jack M. Sasson, *Jonah: A New Translation with Introduction, Commentary, and Interpretation*, The Anchor Bible (New York: Doubleday, 1990), p. 172, cited in Estelle, *Salvation Through Judgment and Mercy*, p. 82.

9. John Calvin, *Institutes of the Christian Religion*, edited by John T. McNeill, translated by Ford Lewis Battles, vol. 1, The Library of Christian Classics (Louisville, KY: Westminster John Knox Press, 2011), p. 516.

10. Samuel Grandy, "I Hear the Accuser Roar" (hymn).

11. C. S. Lewis, *The Four Loves* (New York: Harcourt and Brace, 1960), p. 22.

12. Ibid.

13. Lewis, *Four Loves*, p. 26.

14. Ibid.

15. Lewis, *Four Loves*, p. 29.

16. Lewis, *Four Loves*, p. 27.

17. Some interpreters resist this characterization of Jonah. Some have argued that Jonah's anger has nothing to do with the race or foreignness of the Ninevites, that Jonah was only distressed that any such wicked, violent group of people could be forgiven and not punished.

   Others have countered that Jonah knew that to go to a foreign nation with the message of salvation was part of God's rejection and judgment on Israel (e.g., Deuteronomy 32:15–21). As an example of this view, see Peter Leithart, *A House for My Name: A Survey of the Old Testament* (Moscow, ID: Canon

Press, 2000), pp. 181–82. Leithart argues that when Deuteronomy 32:21 says that God will "provoke" Israel "to jealousy by those who are 'no people,'" it is predicting that God will judge Israel by going to the Gentiles, showing them mercy, and thereby provoking the Jews to "jealousy" in order to win them back to himself. Indeed, Paul quotes Deuteronomy 32:21 in Romans 11:19 and says that this is what God is doing in Christ's time, namely, through the growth of the Christian church. Leithart insists that Jonah in his own day still would have read Deuteronomy 32:21 in the same way that Paul did, even though there is no indication that Jewish teachers before Christ understood the text that way. Leithart's explanation of why Jonah refused to go Nineveh is novel, but it is definitely a minority view.

Another group rightly warns that calling Jonah a racist can itself be an exercise in anti-Semitism. It can be a way of criticizing only Jews, rather than pointing to the universal human propensity for racial bigotry and prejudice.

Nevertheless, the evidence for Jonah's race-tinged nationalism is too strong. Of course it is natural for Jonah to want to see evildoers punished, and it is also completely understandable to worry about the Assyrian capital's threat to Israel. But when Jonah refused a direct order to bring God's message to the Ninevites, he was making a decision to put Israel's national and political interests ahead of God's will. To make your nation and race more important than God is by definition to make them into idols.

There are other indications that the book of Jonah is addressing racist nationalism. Many have pointed out that the entire story very "deliberately gives a sympathetic representation of Gentiles" at every point in the text. Compared to both the pagan sailors in the boat and the Ninevites themselves, Jonah appears ungenerous, cruel, and closed-minded. Allen argues that this appreciative view of nonbelievers and racial outsiders is targeted to a Jewish community "embittered by its legacy of national suffering and foreign opposition." Leslie C. Allen, *The Books of Joel* (Grand Rapids, MI: Wm. B. Eerdmans, 1976), p. 191.

It is important, however, to see that it is not only Jonah who is critiqued for his racism, xenophobia, and nationalism. God is also condemning the Ninevites for their imperialism, oppression, and social injustice. As we have noted, the Assyrians were not being called by God at this point to stop worshipping idols and start worshipping him. Jonah's message was a call to do justice, just as Amos preached to the nations (Amos 1:1–2:3). God tells the pagan nations to stop their violence against the weak and the poor. The text, then, calls out injustice and nationalism on all sides.

18. Paul Tillich, *Dynamics of Faith* (New York: HarperOne, 2009). He writes that to have no deity or god would be "to remain unconcerned about the meaning of one's existence," and so "God can be denied only in the name of God" (p. 52).

19. David Foster Wallace, "David Foster Wallace in His Own Words" (commencement address, Kenyon College, May 21, 2005), *1843*, September 19, 2008, http://moreintelligentlife .com/story/david-foster-wallace-in-his-own-words. See also a printed version in Dave Eggers, *The Best Nonrequired Reading 2006*, 1st ed. (Wilmington, MA: Mariner Books, 2006), pp. 355–64.

20. John Newton, *Olney Hymns*, 1779, quoted in J. I. Packer, *Knowing God* (Downers Grove, IL: InterVarsity Press, 1973), p. 229.

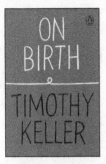
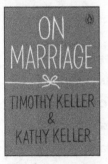
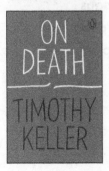

ALSO AVAILABLE

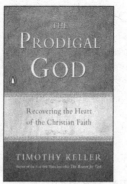

REDISCOVERING JONAH

GOD'S WISDOM FOR NAVIGATING LIFE

HIDDEN CHRISTMAS

MAKING SENSE OF GOD

THE SONGS OF JESUS

PREACHING

PRAYER

ENCOUNTERS WITH JESUS

WALKING WITH GOD THROUGH PAIN AND SUFFERING

EVERY GOOD ENDEAVOR

THE MEANING OF MARRIAGE

JESUS THE KING

GENEROUS JUSTICE

COUNTERFEIT GODS

THE PRODIGAL GOD

THE REASON FOR GOD